SILICON VALLEY STORIES

SILICON VALLEY STORIES

STARTUPS, STORIES, AND LESSONS LEARNED

ADAM BEGUELIN, PHD

NEW DEGREE PRESS

COPYRIGHT © 2020 ADAM BEGUELIN, PHD

All rights reserved.

SILICON VALLEY STORIES

Startups, stories, and lessons learned

ISBN	978-1-64137-441-5	*Paperback*
	978-1-64137-442-2	*Kindle Ebook*
	978-1-64137-443-9	*Ebook*

To Em, it's been a wild ride.

CONTENTS

CHAPTER 0.   NOTE FROM THE AUTHOR   13

1. ACADEMIC DAYS   **23**
CHAPTER 1.   EMORY   25
CHAPTER 2.   BOULDER   33

2. INKTOMI DAYS   **43**
CHAPTER 3.   INKTOMI INTERVIEW DAY   45
CHAPTER 4.   AOL DINNER   55
CHAPTER 5.   THE TAX THING   59
CHAPTER 6.   HOW DOES IT FEEL?   65
CHAPTER 7.   HABANERO BURGER   75
CHAPTER 8.   PAPER MILLIONAIRE   83

3. TRUVEO DAYS   **91**
CHAPTER 9.   RED SWOOSH   93
CHAPTER 10.   TRUVEO BEGINS   101
CHAPTER 11.   JIGSAW OFFICES   115
CHAPTER 12.   HAWAII CODING   119
CHAPTER 13.   DON'T DROP THAT DATA   123

4. POST ECONOMIC DAYS   **129**

CHAPTER 14.   CLUBHOUSE   131

EPILOGUE   WHERE ARE THEY NOW?   141

EARLY CONTRIBUTORS   151

APPENDIX   153

You need three things to become a successful novelist: talent, luck and discipline. Discipline is the one element of those three things that you can control, and so that is the one that you have to focus on controlling, and you just have to hope and trust in the other two.

— MICHAEL CHABON

TIMELINE

1981 – 1985 Emory University, BS in Mathematics and Computer Science

1985 – 1990 University of Colorado, PhD in Computer Science

1990 Paris Postdoc

1991 – 1992 Tennessee Postdoc

1992 – 1996 Carnegie Mellon University, Computer Science Faculty

1996 – 2001 **Inktomi (IPO 1998, $25B 2000)**

2001 **Centrata / NeoPyx*** / Retirement 1

2002 **Red Swoosh**

2002 – 2003 Oracle (Inktomi acquired by Yahoo! in 2003 for $0.241B)

2003 – 2004 Macrovision

2004 – 2005 **Truveo*** (Acquired by AOL)

2006 – 2007 AOL

2007 – 2009 Retirement 2

2010 – 2014 **Sensr.net***

2014 – 2015 Retirement 3

2015 – 2016 **Dynamite Labs***

2017 – Present Retirement 4 (Not really retired...)

* Co-founder

Other related dates

1995
Netscape IPO

1996
Lycos IPO
Yahoo! IPO
Excite IPO

1997
@Home IPO

1998
Inktomi IPO

2003
Yahoo! acquires Inktomi

2010
Salesforce acquires Jigsaw

CHAPTER 0

NOTE FROM THE AUTHOR

———

1999, San Mateo, California

"Our stock is worth $50 million dollars now," my wife said excitedly, doing a little dance in the kitchen of our tiny California rancher.

"No way," I said. "That can't be right."

She showed me the numbers. Wow. Sure enough, Inktomi stock was at an all-time high, something that happened again and again. I had been with the company for almost three years and had several stock grants at this point, all given to me before the IPO (Initial Public Offering). At the beginning we had thought those options might net us maybe a million dollars, but no way did we think they would be worth over $50 million. This was crazy.

I started to panic a little. What should we be doing with all that money? A new house, cars, and a trip to Hawaii were already flashing through my mind despite my disbelief. Everyone has heard stories of lottery winners who get rich and then ruin their lives. I didn't want to go down that path. Part of me also didn't believe it was real. In a sense, it wasn't. Stock options are not cash in the bank, they are the ability to buy stock at a certain price and then sell that stock. Stock could go up or down. We were used to Inktomi stock going up and up, but of course that could change.

As anyone who has read a mutual fund prospectus knows: Past performance is no guarantee of future results.

* * *

Inktomi had started as a research project in the Computer Science Department at UC Berkeley. Professor Eric Brewer was running the Berkeley NOW project. NOW stood for Network of Workstations. The idea was to connect standard workstations (basically high-powered PCs) and turn them into a supercomputer. If you want to prove that you've built a supercomputer, you need to use that supercomputer to solve some big problem. Eric and his grad student Paul Gauthier thought web search was that big problem.

The web seemed big, even in 1995. And it was growing fast, very fast. Paul set off to build a web search engine using the NOW technology. They named it Inktomi after the mythical Lakota Indian spider spirit. If you're going to rule the web, you might as well have a spider spirit on your side. It was also a bit of a joke—spiders and webs go together, of course.

Inktomi turned into a $25 billion company in four years. By comparison, Google today, after twenty years, is worth around $830 billion. Clearly Inktomi was onto something. But, after only six years, Inktomi as a company no longer existed. The company focused on providing tools to build the internet and got caught up in that mania. When the mania was over, the bottom dropped out of that market, taking Inktomi down with it. Explosive growth followed by destructive crashes makes for crazy stories.

I had a front row seat to this roller coaster ride. In the early 1990s I was a researcher at Carnegie Mellon University working on something called PVM (Parallel Virtual Machine). PVM was a toolkit for connecting computers together to solve a single problem. In the research world at the time, PVM was a cousin to the Berkeley NOW project. I knew some of the Inktomi folks through the research community, which led to me being recruited as an early employee in 1996. That was a busy year. Yahoo! went public in 1996. Hotmail was launched in 1996. Lycos (another search spider) had their IPO in 1996. The dot-com frenzy was just beginning.

After I joined, the company grew from around twenty people to a Wall Street darling with a $25 billion market cap by 2000. In the heady days of the late '90s, Inktomi powered the big guys: AOL, Microsoft, and Yahoo! all used Inktomi technology. That team of twenty or so folks rose to over a thousand ecstatic employees, all holding stock options. The company generated paper billionaires and scores of paper millionaires. Some walked away with more treasure than they ever imagined. Others were left abandoned, empty handed, and unemployed as the world moved on. Eventually Inktomi was acquired by Yahoo! in 2003 for only $241 million.

* * *

Silicon Valley has undoubtedly changed the world. The dotcom craziness that started with Netscape's IPO in 1995 and perhaps finished with the bankruptcy of Worldcom and Enron was just the beginning. Today the heart of Silicon Valley has moved slightly north from Palo Alto to San Francisco, where homeless drug addicts live on the streets outside the offices of internet powerhouses like Google and Twitter. In those shiny towers, millionaire software engineers sip their company provided cappuccinos (or maybe kombucha) while creating products that entice and entertain.

Billions of dollars per year are invested in startups. In 2018 alone, 8,383 venture-backed companies raised more than $130 billion.[1] This is indeed big business. Everyone knows the behemoths of Silicon Valley, but these are the outliers, the winners of the evolutionary system of startups, entrepreneurs, and venture capitalists that make up Silicon Valley. How are these companies created, and what motivates the people involved? What happens to the ones that fail? What happens to the winners and losers of this game? This book answers these questions.

I've seen startups created and destroyed in the primordial soup of Silicon Valley entrepreneurship. I've seen people

---

1   Bobby Franklin, "How big was 2018 for VC? Historic." Venture Beat, January 12, 2019.

who've made it, those who gave up, and many who are still trying. Why is Silicon Valley so alluring? How does it work? What motivates people to get involved and pour their hearts and minds into creating companies? In the end, what do folks get out of it? One friend of mine likes to say, "He who dies with the most stories wins." This book is about those stories.

I didn't start out on the path to entrepreneurship. I was an academic who liked writing code and building software as a research project, not for sale or for profit. For me the fun came from thinking up something useful and novel and trying to bring that thing into reality. I was frustrated that my work wasn't really appreciated in the academic world. It wasn't theoretical enough. I got a thrill out of people using software I helped create, but there wasn't much academic value in having a user group for new software.

Moving to Silicon Valley changed that. Having users is what it's all about. Having paying customers is even better. Instead of writing research papers and trying to impress other academics, I started building software people paid for. This was real validation. Making an impact meant building software that changed people's lives. At Inktomi we built software that at one point processed 40 percent of the world's web traffic. That was cool.[2]

I've worked at seven Silicon Valley tech startups and co-founded four. I've had two exits, one IPO, and one acquisition. That's almost a 30 percent hit rate, so not bad by Silicon

---

2   Brian Totty, 2020. User Profile, LinkedIn, accessed February 6, 2020.

Valley standards where conventional wisdom tells us that nine out of ten startups fail. People think joining a startup is a surefire way to get rich. The odds are against you, but it does happen. This book is about the hits and the misses and how people respond.

I've tried to retire three times, once in my thirties, once in my forties, and finally in my fifties when I realized I'll never really retire, not in the traditional sense of the word. Each time, I missed the camaraderie and excitement of the startup. We had weird traditions like water gun fights in the office, Habanero Burger challenges, and the hanging of the pig. Strange art like a Big Boy statue rescued from a restaurant and a Tiki head reminded us of our beginnings.

Along with the camaraderie, I missed the task of figuring something out, like a puzzle. If we can just fit the pieces together correctly, we can make something new that will change the world and make us all a wealthy return. There are certainly mixed motivations when doing a startup. The lure of wealth is one, but for me it was the excitement of building something and working with smart people to do it.

After my second exit, I was sure I was ready to retire. My wife and I moved to Saigon, and we put the kids in international schools. I was ready to learn Vietnamese and spend my time doing whatever I wanted. I exercised a little and ate too much. I wrote a blog about my experiences. I tried learning new programming languages and working on coding projects. I met new people and thought about joining their businesses. I even rented an office where I could go to "work," but, mainly, I was bored.

People, especially in America, equate wealth with success and happiness. More people get rich in Silicon Valley than perhaps any other place in the world. It's thrilling to start a company with just an idea and some know-how, then turn that into something new that people want to use in their daily lives. I've seen this happen many times and made it work on a couple of occasions.

While no single approach will work for everyone, there are a few standard ways of going about startups, especially in Silicon Valley. If you're smart, lucky, and a hard worker, you may even get rich from one. But don't assume all your problems will be solved by money or that you can kick back on the beach with your piña coladas, watch the sunset, and life will be good. Don't assume that once you're a success, you're done. It doesn't really work that way. Most people don't consider this. They are busy making a living and that distracts them from thinking about what they really want.

What do you do with your life when you don't *have* to do anything with your life? This book is about the crazy stories of hits and misses of Silicon Valley, but it's also about what happens to the people involved. When you strip away the need to work, what are you left with? There are many answers to this question. It's been said that life happens when you're making other plans. Once the need for money is no longer something to worry about, how do you deal with that void? What do you really want to do with your existence? I've struggled with this question my entire life. These are the stories of how some folks have solved this problem.

* * *

I see myself as a misfit with a naïve confidence. In college I was called *Nouveau Riche* by a fellow student who was a trust-fund baby. That stuck with me. I'm sure he meant it as an insult, but a part of me liked the label. I was living in a comfortable world, but I was only one generation removed from immigrant farmers. One of my cousins was a carnie named Poon (not a nickname). My grandparents still had an outhouse, a reminder that indoor plumbing was a new addition. My family believed in education. That's what got my father off the farm and into his own medical practice. That same focus on education opened many doors for me and ultimately led me down the path to Silicon Valley.

In this book you'll see what it's like to be a struggling academic. I started when Computer Science was a fairly obscure field. The world was just starting to understand what could be done with this incredibly flexible technology. When I was a grad student in Computer Science I ran into a girl who was studying Physics and she mocked Computer Science. "Is it *really* a science?" she asked, jokingly. Academics can be snarky. I played the academic game fairly well, reaching the top echelons of the best universities, but ultimately it wasn't the game for me. Perhaps I was still the nouveau-riche kid who overstepped his boundaries. I moved to Silicon Valley where new riches are what it's all about.

In this book you'll experience what it was like to be part of one of the biggest successes (and failures) of the dot-com boom (and bust). Inktomi was the second most successful IPO of 1998 next to eBay.[3] It was one of the most important companies behind the infrastructure of the internet in the late 1990s. Today no one has heard of it. You'll see how Silicon Valley creates companies and what it's like to be a part of that. What is it like to found a company? To start from scratch and build something entirely new? What's it like to sell your creation and see it taken over by corporate America? You'll learn some tips on how it's done and what to do if you're caught up in a startup that's taking off.

You'll see some failures, some non-starters, and some companies that go on like zombies, never quite dying. What's it like to suddenly have more money than you know what to do with? You'll meet characters who took their new wealth and rode off into the sunset and those who can't seem to stop playing the game no matter how much treasure they've accumulated. You'll learn some of the lessons I've gleaned from these experiences. What's really important in life? What's retirement like when the word retirement doesn't fit?

If you're interested in what it's like to make the move from academia to industry, here's a case study. Silicon Valley is a bit like a clubhouse. I'll teach you some of the secret handshakes to help you get in the door. If you're curious about what happened inside companies during the dot-com period or how things work in Silicon Valley, this is the book for you. If you've wondered what people do when they make enough money to live life without working, you'll see many different

---

3   Eric Brewer, "Inktomi's Wild Ride – A Personal View of the Internet Bubble", Computer History Museum, YouTube Video, July 25, 2008.

approaches in these stories. These lessons also apply to life in general. Sudden wealth brings everything to a head. The issues become more crucial and the solutions more creative.

If you're thinking of starting a company or joining a startup, this will give you a glimpse of what it might be like. Every startup is different, but there are many similarities. Most companies follow templates and standard paths. But it's not just about the companies, it's about the people. Should you take a risk? What's the right mix for a happy life? You'll see some common mistakes, mistakes which hopefully you'll avoid should similar situations arise in your life. In the end, Silicon Valley is a place of extremes. Those extremes bring out the best and the worst, and my story is no exception.

And that $50 million? It was mostly on paper, meaning we couldn't sell it due to vesting and company blackout periods. Our main strategy was *sell as you vest*. When you're granted stock options they vest over time. My Inktomi options vested over fifty months, or 2 percent per month. This meant each month I could sell another 2 percent, which we tried to do. When the stock goes up each month, you feel stupid for selling. When it starts crashing, you're glad you sold, but you still secretly regret it, since you hope it will go back up again. In the end, our Inktomi windfall resulted in a nice cushion but not nearly enough to retire, trust me, I tried!

1

ACADEMIC DAYS

CHAPTER 1

EMORY

1981, Emory University, Atlanta Georgia

"Dude, why do you have a computer? Can you play video games on that?"

I arrived at Emory in 1981 with my Apple II. I was the only kid in the dorm with a computer and maybe the only kid in any of the dorms with a computer at that time. I used it to write my college papers and the printer was so crappy most of my professors complained about it. Mostly my friends used it to play computer games. I preferred programming it. If you want to understand programming, you must understand language.

Emory didn't have a Computer Science department, but they had a Mathematics and Computer Science major in the Mathematics Department. I hated calculus and loved programming. To me calculus was an abstraction of the world. Sure it was very useful as a way to solve certain problems. But with programming you could *do something*, not just describe it. You could create something new that behaved how you wanted it to behave. With calculus you could figure out how to build something, or describe how something worked, but you couldn't directly create something with it that immediately functioned in the real world. Creating something new in the world was what excited me about programming.

My first summer at Emory I signed up for Emory in Paris. It was a bit of a shock for me and I didn't get along well with most of the other kids on the trip. I did make a friend with a local Parisian girl. Actually, she was Spanish but lived in Paris. I couldn't really tell her apart from French kids, but I got the feeling she felt like an outsider. I learned a lot about France and enjoyed living in a different country, something I would continue to repeat throughout my life. But the culture stuff didn't really get me excited. I was mostly bored with the complicated French grammar and the lectures on French theater. I learned I enjoyed exploring other cultures, but I was sure a French major wasn't for me.

The summer after my sophomore year I focused on the computer programming language instead of French. That summer I took An Introduction to the C Language. I found C was clean, efficient, and powerful. The professor was Dr. Bykat. He was Russian and this was in the early '80s. Ronald Reagan was in office and there were anti-nuke posters around campus. The cold war seemed to be heating up, and the Russians were the bad guys. Regardless, I liked Dr. Bykat. He was kind of a hardass. He had a pretty strong accent and some kids had trouble understanding him. He was no Dr. Strangelove, but his accent was intriguing.

One day in class he was showing code for an editor. As an example for us, he had written a C program that allowed you to edit text. I noticed a bug that would be triggered under certain circumstances, deleting a line and then trying to move the cursor up after the delete. He was demonstrating the editor in class.

Me: "Dr. Bykat, can you delete that line and then move the cursor up?"

Bykat: "Of course."

He does this and the program crashes. A few gasps and laughs from around the room. Frankly, the students are a little afraid of him and wonder how he'll react to his code crashing up on the screen in front of everyone. He turns and scowls at me, but then breaks into a smile. In his heavy Russian accent, "Very good. A for you." After that I was his favorite student.

When I was choosing an honors thesis as a senior, I first thought about doing something in AI. Then one of my professors, Ken Mandelberg, urged me to think about doing something more practical. This was 1984 and in those days, AI was far from making the impact that it is today. It was mostly theoretical, and it was hard to see that changing anytime soon.

My friend Janice Mirra had graduated a couple years ahead of me, and she had a job running computers at the Emory hospital. I was impressed with her business suits and her real money. I told her I wanted to do my thesis in AI. She scoffed. "Do you really think computers can replace humans?" she challenged.

"Sure, why not?" I was a sci-fi fan. And theoretically, I was sure that computers were not that different from people. If they got fast enough and we figured out how to program them correctly, I was sure they would get there.

"You honestly think a computer could be the CEO of a company? That a program could do what a human does, in a role as complex as that?" She wasn't giving.

"Yes, I think it could happen," I responded, but a lot less sure. She had a point. AI was nowhere near replacing humans, especially in 1984. What she was talking about is now called AGI (Artificial General Intelligence). Today the debate continues, and we're a lot closer to AGI, and computers are driving cars and beating us humans in Go, Chess, and about any game out there. I decided to keep looking for an idea.

While I was searching for a thesis topic, Apple came out with the Macintosh. Apple introduced the world to the Mac in a famous 1984 Superbowl commercial that was eerie and exciting. It was a scene alluding to George Orwell's *1984*, with the population depicted as mindless drones staring and a large screen controlled by Big Brother. Then an athletic woman runs in swinging a sledgehammer and destroys the screen, revealing a bright light that amazes the gathered crowd. An announcer then reads a message on the screen, shown in a beautiful Apple font:

On January 24th, Apple Computer will introduce Macintosh. And you'll see why 1984 won't be like "1984."

This was exciting. This was something practical and real that was changing the world. This is what Dr. Mandelberg was talking about. I had to have one. The original price of the Mac was $2,400. That's about $6,000 in today's dollars, crazy expensive for a computer that couldn't do much. My friend Peter Stephan and I somehow convinced our parents that we should buy Macs. We were both Math and Computer Science majors after all, we needed the latest technology.

It turned out Apple had an educational discount, but you had to buy it from a school that was enrolled in the program. Emory wasn't part of Apple's program, but Georgia Tech was. Georgia Tech would allow Emory students to buy the Macs at the educational discount, as long as we had valid IDs and paid cash. Two Macs with 512MB of memory (called Fat Macs back then) plus a couple printers ran us $6,000, and that was with the student discount. Off we went to a sketchy part of downtown Atlanta with the equivalent of $15,000 in cash in today's dollars. Peter had previously been mugged on campus, and we were particularly nervous. I had the cash stuffed into my front pocket, somehow thinking that was less conspicuous. Luckily we didn't get mugged and made it back to our crappy rental house near the University on Adelia Place. Little did we know, our connection to Silicon Valley was just beginning.

The Mac was amazing at the time. It was the first personal computer that had graphical user interface, including windows and mouse. This was revolutionary. When I first got it home, I spent all night playing around with it. Later I had a dream that I was walking around Emory with a mouse in my pocket that was moving a pointer around in space. I could point and click on people's heads and a little window would pop up where I could see their thoughts! There was something visceral about this technology. This was real. It was new and changing the world.

For my honor's thesis I wrote some software that would open windows on a Mac and spawn a shell process on our campus Unix mainframe. The idea was that each window would be a separate shell on the mainframe. What you typed in one of the Mac windows on your desktop actually ended up controlling a command line interface on the Unix mainframe. It was a cool idea and quite practical if I could get it to work.

The software was complicated to write at the time. Dr. Mandelberg pointed me to a C compiler from Stanford called SUMacC (Stanford University Macintosh C). I actually wrote the code on the mainframe and compiled it there. The mainframe was back at Fishburne Hall, a few miles away on the Emory campus. I was sitting at my homemade desk in my bedroom of our rental house with my new Mac in front of me. I had my waterbed to my right and my fish tank on some shelves to my left.

In what seemed clever at the time, I had placed a Playboy centerfold behind the fish tank for the background. Immature male college dorm chic, for sure. Thinking back, this was a little piece of geek heaven, which foreshadows the scruffy startup digs I would favor in the future, minus the centerfolds. The Mac was connected to a modem that would dial into the university computer, allowing me to move files back and forth between the mainframe and my Mac.

Once I created my "app" on the mainframe, I then had to download it to my Mac to run it. This took several minutes each time. Even longer if one of our roommates decided to pick up the phone and ruin my modem connection.

I would hear an ear piercing modem screeching sound from the dining room, where my roommate Dave Antonez occasionally picked up the other phone extension. "Ah! Dammit, Adam, you're on the phone again!" he would yell.

"You fucker, you just ruined my download," I would shout back. "Now I have to do it all over again. Don't pick up the phone unless you check with me first, I have to get this shit done!"

Ah, the joys of sharing a house with a bunch of college seniors. Again, not so different from a Silicon Valley startup.

The Mac interface was in a language called Pascal. Pascal was a modern language for the time, but it would quickly lose out to C. Apple was good at picking trends, just not always the winning ones. I wrote my app in C, but it had to interface to the Mac by calling Pascal. Confusing, right? In some ways I felt like I was back in Paris trying to interface in French by translating my thoughts from English. In some ways the languages Pascal and French have had the same fate, diminishing in relevance as the world evolves.

There was no debugger or anything like that in those days. At times it was difficult trying to figure out where my program was crashing. In a flash of inspiration, I realized that by adding lines of code to make the computer beep, I could track its progress as it ran. I would then download the program and listen to the number of beeps so I could figure out how far the code was getting before it crashed. Once I knew where it was crashing, I could figure out what was causing the bug.

Today we do something similar called "printline debugging," where you put printline statements in your code to figure out where it's going wrong. I invented beepcount debugging, I suppose. It was a clever hack that allowed me to make progress when I didn't have other options. This sort of ingenuity would serve me well later in life. At startups you're always on the bleeding edge and you often need to improvise to make progress.

I finished the app and wrote up my thesis in time to graduate. During my thesis defense one of the professors asked to see if I could make it crash by opening a ton of windows. I said sure and started opening a bunch of windows. Eventually he got bored when it wouldn't crash and asked me to stop. I had proved my work solid. This scene would repeat itself in various forms over the coming years. A thesis defense in front of a group of professors is not unlike a pitch meeting in front of a group of venture capitalists. In this case, Emory deemed it good enough to award me summa cum laude for the work.

I had my first exit.

CHAPTER 2

BOULDER

1986, CU Engineering Center, Boulder, Colorado

"I think I'm going to catch a matinee this afternoon." It was Friday after all.

Xiaodong chuckled and shook his head. "No. Bad idea."

In the Fall of 1986, I was a teaching assistant at CU Boulder in the CS department. I shared a windowless room in the corner of the engineering building with a handful of other TAs. It was an office, but it felt more like a concrete bunker. We had a few shared ADM3a terminals that were connected to the Unix system we used for email and coding. I was goofing around on the ADM3a and reading the *Daily Coloradan*. It was a Friday, and I was thinking of catching an early movie. And the showtimes before 7 p.m. were cheap. Cost is always important to a low-paid grad student.

"I think I'm going to catch a matinee this afternoon," I said to Xiaodong as he waked into the room. It was Friday after all.

He chuckled and shook his head, "No. Bad idea." He was amazed at the lazy rich American kid who was going to go to the movies when he could be doing something more important.

Xiaodong had come to Boulder from China. He was super smart and a very hard worker. He was also opinionated and not afraid to share his opinions. He thought about things that hadn't really occurred to me. Like how to get a leg up. Sure, we both had TA jobs and it was pretty nice. The university gave us a small salary and paid our tuition. We got a shared office and we got to teach undergrads how to program.

There was something better out there. A step up in the hierarchy. We could be RAs instead of TAs. An RA was a research assistant. You worked for a professor and he paid you out of his research grant. Being an RA meant you could spend your days working on leading edge research problems instead of helping to teach undergrads how to code.

BECOMING A RESEARCHER

Xiaodong said there was a professor who was looking for research assistants and was giving a talk. His name was Warren Burton. He was doing research in parallel and functional programming. I had no idea what that was, but Xiaodong assured me that being an RA instead of a TA was an improvement for which I should strive. Being a research assistant was better than being a teaching assistant. TAs and RAs got the same pay, but RAs got better offices and more flexible schedules.

He convinced me to attend the talk. It was in one of the classrooms (also windowless) in the engineering center on that Friday afternoon. Maybe ten students showed up. Dr. Burton had a research grant to study a new kind of programming called Functional Programming. It was a more mathematical way to write programs. Besides being less error prone, this kind of programming might also make it easier to program parallel computers.

In the race to build ever faster computers, parallel computing was one approach. Companies would build computers with multiple CPUs in one box and the idea was to run programs *in parallel* on those CPUs at the same time. The analogy was like having multiple workers to solve a problem, say, build a house. If you had ten workers, they could build a house ten times faster than a single worker. This meant parallelizing the problem, breaking it down so different parts could be done at the same time, in parallel.

Of course not all problems work this way. Put ten women on the job of having a baby, and you still can't get a newborn in a month. (You can get ten babies in nine months, but that doesn't help if you really need that baby next month.) The point is, figuring out how to write parallel programs was hard and important.

I was intrigued with Dr. Burton and his work. I talked with him after the presentation and he asked me to come by his office the following week for a more in-depth interview. In the end, he made me an offer to be his research assistant starting the next semester. I didn't really realize it at the time, but this choice would send me down a golden path.

Dr. Burton introduced me to the world of academic research. He would have me read academic papers, and then meet him once a week to discuss them. We talked about Functional Programming, recursion, and space filling functions. Of course, I was still taking classes and preparing for the PhD qualifying exams.

Dr. Burton's work was about how to make programming parallel computers easier. Back in the late '80s his research was how to write programs that could be parallelized automatically. The hardware guys were trying different ways to connect multiple processors. There were two camps, shared memory and distributed memory. In either case, you still needed to figure out how to break up your program (your app) so it could run on multiple CPUs at the same time. The hope was with Functional programming, that you could simply describe the problem in a mathematically clean way, and the compiler could figure out how to break up tasks and run them in parallel.

One of his research grants was from Amoco Production Company. They were interested in high performance computing and how to process data faster, so they could find oil more cheaply. Amoco had a research center in Tulsa, Oklahoma, and they were looking for summer interns to come work on their parallel computing projects. Lucky for me, Dr. Burton recommended me for an internship there. Being a grad student with no prospects for the summer, I readily accepted the offer. That summer I moved to Tulsa and was introduced to the world of industrial research.

Amoco had a bunch of different research projects going on. I was assigned to the parallel computing group and given the task of testing out the nCUBE computer. The nCUBE was their latest toy at the lab. It was a distributed memory parallel computer. The connections between the processors used a hypercube topology. This was supposed to be a good general way to connect the processors. There were some research papers about how hypercube networks worked, and we wanted to write some code to test out the hypercube network which was at the heart of the nCUBE computer.

I wrote some code and ran some tests. The results were interesting, so together one of my mentors at the lab and I wrote them up for a conference on Hypercube multiprocessors in October 1986. ("Proceedings of the Second Conference on Hypercube Multiprocessors.") I had my first academic publication!

LOSING FUNDING

During my second summer in grad school, I was working for Amoco again, and I got a fateful email from Dr. Burton. He was leaving Boulder to join the faculty at the University of Utah. He offered to take me along, but I was happy in Boulder. But this also meant the grant money for my RA was disappearing. CU would take me back as a TA again, but that felt like failure, a step backward.

Looking back, this was in some ways a dress rehearsal for Silicon Valley, where scrambling for funds is a normal part of life. I didn't want to move to Utah, and I didn't want to be a TA again. This was toward the end of my second successful summer at Amoco, and I had the feeling they liked my work. I decided to pitch my boss, Rex Page, on the idea of supporting me directly to continue doing research at the university. I was excited when Rex said they would fund me. Like a rich angel investor, Rex threw some money my way, supporting a project that may or may not pay off.

When I contacted the university with the good news that I had a research grant to support myself, they informed me that students couldn't have research grants by themselves. I was a bit miffed at this, but luckily Lloyd Fosdick, the department chair, was willing to be my advisor (since Dr. Burton had left) and the PI (primary investigator) on my grant. It was a bit of an odd situation. I had money to do research but there was no specific direction or plan on what I should be researching exactly, just something related to parallel computing. In some ways this was like trying to come up with startup ideas. I would meet with Lloyd on a weekly basis and pitch him on crazy ideas I had thought up during the week.

Lloyd was a good sport and put up with my ramblings, but I got the feeling his heart wasn't really in it. He was busy running the department and doing his own research. Luckily for both of us, there was another professor who might be a better fit for me. Gary Nutt was a tenured professor who had left the university to work in the industry for a few years, but now had decided to return to academia.

FINDING DIRECTION

Since Gary was returning, he was building up his stable of grad students. Plus our interests were aligned—his research was in distributed computing, which at a high level is very similar to parallel computing. It didn't hurt that I had my own research grant to boot, so he didn't have to pay for me, at least at the beginning.

During his time away, Gary had worked at Xerox Parc. Xerox Parc (a.k.a. Parc) was a magical research lab in Palo Alto, California, the heart of Silicon Valley. Parc is credited with the invention of many things we take for granted today. The idea of using a mouse and windows as a user interface was invented at Parc and later popularized by Apple with the Macintosh and, of course, Microsoft with the Windows operating system.

Gary had access to some open source code that they used for a graphical programming system. Gary gave me my first real programming project. I was tasked with porting the system from the Xerox Parc system to our fancy new Sun Microsystems computers. The department had a grant from Sun, and we had a beautiful lab with these gorgeous computers all lined up facing huge windows looking out over Boulder. I had graduated to a room with a view! Xiaodong had been right, the RA gig definitely trumped the TA job.

The work was challenging too. I took the code from Parc and ported it over to the Sun workstations. It was my first experience working with someone else's code. It also exposed me to the latest operating system technology. The Apple Macintosh that I programmed at Emory was no longer state of the art. Unix and Sun were now at the top of the heap.

Working on that project taught me a lot. This was another example of learning by doing. I was building skills that would serve me well later in life. The key really isn't so much the exact technology that I was learning, but I was learning how to learn. At Emory I had taught myself how to program the Mac. Now I was learning how to program Unix and the Sun windows system. It was hard but satisfying work. I eventually got it to work, honing my skills along the way.

HARDWARE IS HARD

Being poor graduate students, we were always on the lookout for opportunities. Xiaodong and I got word that a parallel computing startup called Topologix was looking for programmers. We both ended up taking part time jobs there. It was my first exposure to the startup world. These guys were building a supercomputer that you could add on to a Sun workstation. It was similar to the nCube computer I had used at Amoco.

"Topologix launched a rocketship that ran head on into the Intel Pentium chip and lost."

The startup digs were nice. I was impressed by the free coffee and tea in the break room. All the full-time developers had fancy desk chairs and their own Sun workstations, which was quite extravagant in those days. The CEO had a fancy M3 BMW that was always parked right outside the entrance to the office. He was known to joke about all the speeding tickets he got racing around between meetings.

A few months into our part-time jobs, we arrived to find the office in disarray. Sally the HR person flagged us down as we entered the office.

"I'm sorry, but we're going to have to let you guys go. The company is shutting down," she said wearily. "You guys can gather up your personal belongings and grab some drinks from the break room. I'll get your final checks ready."

A little surprised, we grabbed our few things we had left at our desks. I was happy not to lose my Led Zeppelin CD. I loved listening to "Houses of the Holy" on repeat while coding.

I ran into Jack, the lead programmer in the break room. "Man, I'm sorry to hear about the company. I'm really surprised. Things seemed to be going so well."

Jack was the resident guru, basically in charge of all things software. "Moore's law is a bitch. The new Pentium just came out and we can't compete."

Wrangling code to get it to work on the Topologix board was a lot of work. Now that Intel had released their new chips, it just wasn't worth all the extra effort to run code on this custom board when you could just buy a new PC with the latest Intel Inside.

"What are you going to do next?" I asked. He seemed pretty cheery for a guy who was losing his job.

"They are giving the full-time folks three months' severance. I get to keep my workstation, so that's cool. I'm now an expert in Solaris device drivers and that's a pretty marketable skill these days. Our Sun Microsystems rep said he would put in my resumé there. Word is they are hiring like crazy. I think I'll take a stint at a big company for a while." He thought for a minute. "At least the hours will be more reasonable. My wife will be happy to have me around more."

The other employees were bummed but it didn't seem that bad. Everyone was optimistic that they could simply find a new job pretty easily.

I wonder if the CEO was able to keep his M3.

2

INKTOMI DAYS

CHAPTER 3

INKTOMI
INTERVIEW DAY

———

October 1996, Carnegie Mellon University, Pittsburgh, Pennsylvania

"We've got a scrappy little startup out here in Berkeley that's working on some very exciting things, perhaps things that could change the world."

In October 1996, I got a well-crafted email from Todd Brin. "We've got a scrappy little startup out here in Berkeley that's working on some very exciting things, perhaps things that could change the world." Would I like to be a part of it?

At that point I had been on the faculty at Carnegie Mellon University for four years. I was a research professor and had my own DARPA contract. DARPA is the Defense Advanced Research Projects Agency—these guys brought us the internet by funding Computer Science research back in the '60s.

While having a DARPA contract to do research is a big deal, that alone won't keep you employed at a top university.

I had the feeling I wasn't doing great at CMU, and I would be out of a job before too long. I didn't have a lot of publications, and my research wasn't making a big impact. Around the time of the email, I had had various meetings with more senior folks in the department who were trying to give me guidance. If you've ever worked at a big company, you may know that there are certain procedures to firing someone. Part of that process includes some well-documented meetings where expectations are very explicitly set. These meetings had that sort of feel.

A great academic knows not only how to wow the graybeards but also bring in the grant money. I was a bit of a conundrum for the department. I brought in the money, but my work didn't have the academic flair that resulted in publications or academic kudos. They suggested I become a DARPA program manager, and I researched what it was all about. Basically you switch sides and decide which research to fund.

This was a very intense job and very political. It was a government position that entailed a lot of power over where big money was spent on academic institutions. You would hear all the latest research and try to figure out what could make an impact, and then you would fight for those programs. It was a stable government job with nice government benefits.

I liked the idea of being in the center of all the action. There was definitely a Star Chamber feel around the DARPA guys. But I didn't like the fact I wouldn't be part of the action, more of a facilitator than a doer. The Inktomi job seemed like the opposite of the DARPA job. With Inktomi, I'd be on the ground making something new and exciting. That said, Inktomi was risky and underfunded. At this time my wife Loan was six months pregnant with our first child, and we were in the middle of renovating a house we had just bought. It didn't seem like the ideal time to change jobs or move across the country.

But Loan is very adventuresome and entrepreneurial. She and her family had escaped Vietnam on a decrepit overloaded boat after the fall of Saigon. They came to America with nothing and rebuilt their lives. Her risk tolerance was in a whole different category from mine.

As a child she saw explosions on the streets of Saigon. She had seen her family risk it all by moving halfway around the world to a very foreign country where they didn't know the culture or the language. She had experienced extreme risks in her life and seemed to take it all in stride. She has an innately positive attitude that things will work out.

That said, risk wasn't completely foreign to me either. I had grown up around risks, perhaps more subtle risks, but risks, nonetheless. My father had a very successful medical practice, but he had an entrepreneurial streak. He started a string of businesses, most of which failed, but the success of his medical practice carried us through these downturns without much problem. It taught me that failure is a very real part of risk, to be careful of your limits. Loan encouraged me to check it out, despite the fact we had several big projects in the works.

Amy Hanlon was the perky redheaded twenty-five-year-old head of HR for Inktomi. Her enthusiasm and resourcefulness reflected that of her employer. She arranged my visit and my travel. This was 1996 and you could buy airline tickets from people on the internet. The tickets were still paper. I got the ticket via FedEx, and it still had some other guy's name on it. Amy assured me it wouldn't be a problem.

In today's post-9/11 world, this seems particularly sketchy. It was a risk, but what was the worst that could happen? They wouldn't let me on the plane? I flew out to SFO and rented a car and drove to Berkeley and checked into my hotel. I didn't know it then, but the next day would change my life forever.

* * *

I arrived early to the Inktomi office, so I headed across the street to the Sonoma Valley Bagel Company. I had never been to Berkeley; the weather was great, fresh, and sunny. Could it be an omen of things to come? Over my coffee and bagel, I thought over what Todd had told me. The search engine was only one of the first products Inktomi would produce. What else could they be cooking up?

They had a great start on search at that point. In May 1996, *HotWired* (the predecessor of *Wired Magazine*) launched HotBot, a search engine powered by Inktomi.[4] HotBot impressed the world by having very fresh results. They could crawl the entire internet weekly, making sure the search

---

4   Wikipedia, s.v. "HotBot," last modified November 19, 2019, 13:38.

results were the latest and greatest. This sort of deal is called white labeling.

Inktomi provided the back-end technology for search, but the front-end design and branding was controlled by other companies. HotBot was Inktomi's first search white-label deal, and it was well received. Inktomi had received amazing press, being known as the search engine with the biggest (50 million pages) and most up-to-date (weekly) index of the entire web. However, they didn't think search was a big enough market. Search seemed important, but it wasn't obvious in 1996 it would be as huge as it is today.

At that time there were other ways of finding things on the internet. Yahoo! had an index built by humans and it was the most important website of the times. Inktomi's underlying NOW (network of workstations) technology could be applied to more problems than just search. Their strategy was to provide multiple internet infrastructure products.

I had no idea what the next product might be. Search seemed like an exciting new business. I couldn't wait to find out what they might be working on. It could be something revolutionary or a total waste of time. Since nine out of ten startups fail and they already had what seemed like a successful product, why risk adding something else? In the end, that risk paid off.

It turns out they were working on a high-performance proxy cache. In those days the internet was growing like crazy, and there seemed to be no end in sight. From 1995 to 2000 the number of users on the internet grew from 16 million to over 300 million.[5] Today we're at 4.5 billion users on the internet. The frictionless economy and irrational exuberance were around the corner, but right then, bandwidth was a big problem, as the network had much more demand than the actual pipes could supply.

Netscape had a blockbuster IPO the year before. On opening day in August 1995, Netscape stock more than doubled from $28 to close at $58.25 after peaking at $74.75. The sixteen-month-old company was worth around $3 billion without having any profit on the books.[6] Things were starting to get crazy. A proxy cache was a great idea. It was a software solution that could make the internet scale better and seem faster to the end user.

A proxy cache is software that runs on a server in the middle of the network and speeds up the network by caching parts of the web so they are stored closer to the user. Today they are an integral part of the internet. In 1996, few people were using them, and no one had a really good one. Inktomi was going to build a super-fast, super-efficient proxy cache and sell the software to internet infrastructure companies like @Home, AOL, and even Enron.

There was a huge demand for the caching product, and it made Inktomi much more money than search ever did, but in the end that market would have a dramatic collapse, taking Inktomi down with it. At the peak, Inktomi was making 60 percent of its revenue from caching. However, revenue went

---

5   Internet Growth Statistics, accessed on February 6, 2020.
6   Alex Planes. "The IPO That Inflated the Dot-Com Bubble." Motley Fool. August 9th, 2013.

from $80 million to $40 million in a single quarter when the telecom market started to fall apart.[7]

* * *

I thought I might end up being a millionaire if this whole startup thing worked out. I knew people got rich doing startups, but I didn't know the details. I also knew my professor salary wouldn't cut it in California. We had a good life in Pittsburgh where I could afford a big house. Most importantly, we had a baby daughter on the way. Was putting everything at risk worth it? For a scrappy startup with no real revenue at the time?

At that point only about twenty people were working there. I met with most of the key engineering staff. Everyone seemed very excited, very smart, but also very fun. At the end of the day, they decided to make me an offer. Jerry Kennelly was the new CFO. He sat me down to present me with my offer. He led with the stock, which was 50,000 shares. Naïvely I didn't understand that this was very generous for employee twenty something. My PhD in Computer Science and CMU pedigree was paying off.

But the salary didn't impress me. I didn't know it at the time, but this is standard procedure for startups. You offer below market salaries, since employees stand to make out like bandits should the company have an IPO and the price of the stock rockets. Employees support the company with

---

7   Eric Brewer, "Inktomi's Wild Ride – A Personal View of the Internet Bubble", Computer History Museum, YouTube Video, July 25, 2008.

low salaries and get compensated later if all goes well. Of course, early-stage startups often fail, then the under compensated employees end up with smaller bank accounts for their efforts. It's a gamble. Conventional wisdom tells us it's worth it.

Even if you don't make money off the company's stock, you're getting valuable startup experience, which can lead to a better job at the next startup or perhaps a bigger, more stable company. If this company doesn't take off, you'll be better equipped to make the next one a success. This is mostly true. If you're skilled enough to join a startup, those skills are highly marketable. If things go down the tubes, you'll be able to land somewhere else. While this is particularly true when the economy is humming along, it will be tougher when the entire market crashes, like it did in 2000.

After the dot-com crash, Silicon Valley emptied out. There is a corridor along Highway 101 from San Mateo down to Palo Alto known for billboards with ads for tech companies. In the good times, these billboards are filled with ads from tech companies, sometimes taunting each other. It's not uncommon for a billboard in front of Oracle to be used by a competitor to throw insults at the software giant. However, in the years after the crash, these billboards had a different flavor, pushing very different products, like beer and fast food. For a while, Silicon Valley became the valley of Budweiser, but it didn't last long.

Of course, I didn't know any of this at the time. I just knew that the salary seemed low. I called my wife and we decided that the salary just wasn't enough. I pushed back. After a lot of uncomfortable back and forth, the Inktomi folks decided to increase the salary, but with one caveat—I sign the offer letter that day! After yet another call to my very pregnant wife back in Pittsburgh, I signed.

Little did I know the company didn't have enough money to make payroll three months out. There are always unseen risks, especially when joining a startup. You can do your homework and still miss red flags. Sometimes it's best not to have all the facts and go with your gut.

When I was granted those shares they were worth $0.30 per share, or about $15,000 in total. As Inktomi stock grew, the company split the stock twice, so my 50,000 shares became 200,000 shares. Companies sometimes do stock splits if the stock gets too high. Basically they double the number of shares while cutting the price in half. It's more of a psychological thing. Financially holding 100 shares at $1,000 per share is no different from holding 200 shares worth $500. Both are worth $100,000. During the dot-com days this was common; it helped mask the fact that companies were becoming overvalued.

In my case, those stock options were worth much more than the few thousand dollars of additional salary I negotiated that day. If I had sold all of them at the peak market cap of $241 per share, which wasn't possible, they would have been worth almost $50 million.

CHAPTER 4

AOL DINNER

Morton's Steak House, May, 1998

Reston, Virginia

Inktomi had two main businesses, Search and Network Products. Search everyone understands, it's what Google is famous for today. Network Products was more obscure, but at the time much more profitable. We created Traffic Server to make the internet faster and better. TS was a high performance proxy cache. It was (still is) software that sits in the network and keeps track of web requests that come through. It keeps copies of objects out on the web, and if multiple users ask for the same object, the later requests are served from the cache instead of being pulled from across the internet. If a thousand AOL users want to read that same article on the *NY Times* page, TS would make sure only one copy was pulled over from the *NY Times* web server. At a high level this makes browsing the internet faster for the end user and cheaper for the ISP, Internet Service Provider. In 1998, AOL was one of the biggest ISPs out there.

Inktomi was powering search at a number of the top websites in 1998, Yahoo!, AOL, and MSN. We needed to prove that our Network Products division was also a big deal. The mantra at Inktomi was we made tools that made the internet work. The idea was that when there is a gold rush going on, you should sell tools to the miners. We thought this was a clever approach and also a safer approach. We knew the internet was going to be huge, so being a key player in the internet infrastructure seemed like a safe and lucrative bet.

AOL was one of the biggest ISPs in 1998. They knew caching was critical to their business and had been using an open source cache in their network. We had to convince them Traffic Server was better than Squid, the free software they were using at the time. This was a great test for us, and we passed with flying colors. When they tested TS they found we could handle twice the traffic Squid could handle. This meant they could turn off half their servers if they switched to TS. Or more importantly, they would be able to double the number of users they could handle for the same price.

We went through a long and difficult trial to get AOL on board. They were using a different version of Unix than we were. This meant we had to port TS from Sun computers to DEC computers. They were similar but not the same. AOL had a unique architecture for their caching, so we had to implement special features that were unique to AOL. Generally, you don't want to spend too much time building custom features since you can't sell those to other customers. But for AOL we made an exception; it was worth it.

AOL wanted to have support engineers on staff at their head-quarters. We were based in Silicon Valley, and AOL was based in DC. We had to build up support staff in DC, and not just regular support but high level engineers who could fix bugs and recompile the software if there were a crisis. In the end we made it. We convinced AOL our product was better, and that it was worth it for them to buy Traffic Server. Our sales guys were excited and in the end, it meant we could move forward toward our IPO.

PARTY TIME

We were stuffed. Michael Askay, the lead sales guy for the AOL deal, was buying dinner for the entire team. Of course, he was expensing it. Anything we wanted, steak, lobster, whatever. This was the celebration dinner. AOL had finally placed the order, $30 million for unlimited licenses for Traffic Server. The sales guys were jubilant and, to show their appreciation, they were taking out the entire AOL engineering team plus a few key Inktomi folks. Peter and I were included. Peter would be our staff engineer embedded at AOL to make sure everything went smoothly. I oversaw the development team back in San Mateo.

You put thirty geeks in a banquet room at Morton's Steak-house and tell them they can have anything and things start adding up quickly. The appetizers arrived like there was no tomorrow. Full dinners were ordered, surf and turf, filet mignon, hanger steaks, porterhouse, maybe the occasional salad. The wine was flowing like water. Mark Meuhl, the head of the team at AOL, wanted the magnum of wine that decorated the entrance to the banquet room. It wasn't really for sale, but Askay negotiated something and soon the huge bottle of wine was being poured for everyone. Of course, diet cokes were ordered to round things out.

After we stuffed our faces for dinner, it was time for the after dinner drinks. Port was a favorite in those days, then someone noticed the most expensive drink on the menu was Louis XIII Cognac for $113 a glass. Being engineers we wanted to optimize our returns—if you're getting something for free off a menu, you might as well order the most expensive thing. As the waitress got halfway around the table it became clear that almost everyone had to try it.

In the end the bill must have been astronomical, but it was nothing compared to the stock market returns that this deal helped enable. Now that Inktomi had AOL as a key customer, the path to our IPO was clear. It would be the second most successful IPO of 1998, just behind eBay. Within two years the company would be worth over $25 billion, and that's a lot of Louis XIII cognac.

CHAPTER 5

THE TAX THING

When you make a lot of money at once, you pay a good chunk of that in taxes. As we approached the IPO at Inktomi, most of the employees were in a situation where they would have the option to make a lot of money very shortly. I remember an internal company talk where our CFO, Jerry Kennelly, gave us a primer on taxes and capital gains. You see normal income like wages are taxed at the highest rate. For those of us who lived in California at the time, the highest tax rate for wages approached 50 percent, once you add state and federal taxes.

The beauty of investing in stocks, however, is that gains on stocks are typically taxed at a lower rate, often the rate goes lower if you hold the stock for a while. This is known as the long-term capital gains rate. It has varied over the years, but the rate was something like 10 or 15 percent in 1998. Of course, most employees at a startup don't actually own stock, they own stock options. That is the option to buy a share of stock at a specific price. Say you join the company when the stock is worth $0.10 and then four years later it's worth $100.10, you can buy that share for $0.10 and immediately sell it for

$100.10, a profit of $100. The problem with that scenario is that you have to pay short-term capital gains on that sale, which means about half your money goes to taxes.

Now imagine a room full of eager employees who have been thinking of this magic number in their heads, the value of their stock. They know they have X number of shares which cost them almost nothing, but soon after the IPO those shares will be worth a lot. They all have some number in their heads, say $100,000 or maybe $1,000,000. Now Jerry is telling them that number is likely to be half of what they think it is. That new house or BMW that was within reach now seems a bit farther away.

But there is good news! You can get that long-term capital gains rate if you buy your stock now and hold it for a year. There are some complications of course. But essentially that's the trick. If you buy your stock options (a.k.a. exercising your options), then you can start that capital gains clock. When that clock hits one year, your tax rate on sale of that stock goes down. When it hits two years it goes down even further. There are even some obscure IRS rules around stock grants, where you can count the grant date into the formula somehow and treat some of your shares as purchased on the grant date, even if you purchased them later. There were some very highly paid tax accountants who could help you with that math, should it be worth your while.

Now you have a one – or two-year period where you must wait. That can be excruciating, but it could also be fatal. There is another "gotcha" here. What if the stock goes down? Let's say you're waiting for a year or two so you can save 20 percent in taxes, then the stock drops 80 percent.

I got lucky at Inktomi. I exercised my unvested options and started those long-term holding clocks. As we waited, the stock just kept going up.

The downside is you must buy the options with cash. Inktomi was gracious and would take a promissory note in lieu of payment should you want to exercise the option and found yourself short of cash. There is, of course, the risk that the IPO will not happen, or that the stock will be worth less after the IPO than what you paid for it when you bought it. These are all real risks.

They didn't happen for the folks that started at Inktomi in the early years. We were lucky and none of these bad things happened to the folks in that room. But certainly a few years later for other option grants or at other companies, early exercise was something that went very, very wrong. We used cash to exercise our options, and it saved us a lot in taxes. In retrospect, a more conservative thing to do would have been to take a promissory note. If the shit hit the fan, then we wouldn't have been out the cash.

I heard of people who exercised their stock options in order to start this process, and then the stock went down below their option price. A worst case scenario is when you buy your options when the option price is below the current stock price and have to pay tax on the difference between the option and the current stock price. The IRS sees this as a gain even though you don't get any cash out of the deal.

Say your option is at $100, and the stock is at $150. When you exercise the option at $100 the IRS sees a gain of $50 even though just bought the option, you didn't sell anything. Now while you're holding this stock, you're hoping it will go to $250, so in a year you can sell and have a gain of $150 and pay the lower tax rate. What happens if the stock goes down below your initial purchase price? Now you paid taxes on a phantom gain. Even worse, the stock could go to zero. Now you've paid taxes and in the end had nothing to show for it.

When we're talking about one share, it doesn't seem so bad. But stock option grants can involve tens of thousands of shares. On a 50,000 share grant, a $100 per share loss could be $5 million. Needless to say, it pays to be careful here.

One way to think about this is to sell enough to have a nice bonus and pay the taxes on that sale. If the stock goes up or down, you locked in a nice gain.

The exercise early trick worked so well for us that I was happy to spread the word to other entrepreneurs at other startups over the years. After Inktomi, when I interviewed at other startups and things got serious, I would ask about early exercise of options. Lucky for me, I never did it again. The post-Inktomi startups I joined as an employee never had an exit. The one I founded did have an exit, but it turns out the founder's shares aren't options, so this isn't an issue.

How could this go wrong? Well it turns out when you exercise your stock options, the difference between the option price (what you pay) and the current fair market value is taxable. So let's say your option price was $0.10 and when you exercised the internal company price was $0.60 per share. That means even if you don't sell, that $0.50 gain is taxable. It turns out that the IRS gives you some leeway here. You get a certain amount of that kind of gain tax free. It was something like $45,000 in 1998. This means if your "unrealized gain" from exercising your options is under $45,000 then you don't need to pay any tax.

But let's say you had a lot of stock and the delta was large, it's possible you could be hit with a very large tax bill. Worse, you may not be able to sell your stock to pay the tax. If the company hasn't had an IPO, then you can't sell, and you're stuck. If the company has gone public, but the stock tanked, then you're doubly screwed. You owe tax on a phantom gain, but the actual investment is now a loss, so selling the stock doesn't help much since it's not worth very much. But guess what? You still owe the taxes.

The key here is not to get too greedy. If you're paying taxes, then that's good, it probably means that you're making money. Don't try to jump through too many crazy hoops to avoid taxes. Sure, take some reasonable precautions, but if things get too complex, they may not be worth it, and they may even end up costing you a lot.

CHAPTER 6

HOW DOES IT FEEL?

——

Inktomi IPO, June 11, 1998

San Mateo, California

After working at Inktomi for a while, I had this nagging question in the back of my head. How much will that stock be worth? When I first started at Inktomi, I didn't really appreciate that the stock was the real reason to work there. For me it was about a new adventure, being paid a decent salary, and working with smart people on important problems. It's cliché now, but we really did believe we were changing the world. We knew the internet was important. We were building the tools that made the internet scale. It would turn out that, at one point, Inktomi software would process 40 percent of all web traffic.

Learning and building were the things I liked. When I arrived, the search product was already up and running. We used a piece of technology there that we called the IoCore. It allowed the programs we wrote to connect to thousands of servers at once and move data around the network very efficiently.

This was a cool new idea being worked on by John Plevyak when I arrived at Inktomi. John was another Computer Science PhD. Inktomi was very good at collecting PhDs. John turned down a job offer to be a professor at UC Davis to join Inktomi in the summer of 1996. He is one of those high-strung savants. He gets hyper-excited about technology. He can also code faster than almost anyone I've met. Just talking to John about coding projects is exhilarating.

He started on the crawler technology that was used in search and then moved over to work on the caching product. The idea that we could develop hyper efficient ways to move lots of data around the network was alluring. To build a search engine, you need to crawl the entire internet and index all the web pages out there. Doing so efficiently was a competitive advantage. It turns out a proxy cache needs the same underlying technology.

It's cool when you can distill down some useful ideas and then figure out multiple ways to leverage them. This was part of the fun in doing a startup. Brainstorming cool ideas and making them happen, then putting those ideas to work in products that change the world.

This lent the work a feeling of purpose. What we were doing mattered. When I was an academic, the goal was to come up with novel ideas that moved science forward. That sounded exciting but, in reality, it wasn't very tangible. Doing a startup is tangible. If you are doing it correctly, you're building things that are not only novel but also that customers are using right away. Customers are demanding your product. They are using it in critical parts of their businesses. The validation piece was missing for me in my academic research. At Inktomi, the validation was real. Millions of people were using our technology daily. Those cool ideas we had made a real impact.

Of course, once you get to the point that your cool idea is being used by millions, this also means it's big business. There are companies that rely on your software. Inside Inktomi we had the engineering team where we created the magic, but we started growing other teams as well.

The sales team to sell the software, and a marketing team to advertise what we were doing. We added documentation and support teams to help our customers understand and use our software better. It was no longer just a group of us geeks above the Sees Candy store in Berkeley toying with obscure ideas on how to build software; we had turned into a real company with real products and real customers. By now our very real investors were now excited that their investments were looking like they would pay off.

Once you realize the scope of your position—how many people are invested—the influence of what you're doing becomes clear. It becomes much more than solving the puzzle for the fun of it. There's much more on the line than fun. Investors have money riding on your idea. They expect revolutionary changes. While this pressure is intense, this pressure is also exciting, but in a new way.

That's when you realize the fuel that makes the machine really move is equity, stock. The investors gave us money so we could build something that would be worth much, much more than the money they gave us. The intellectual challenge, the daily puzzle solving, the team building and cajoling, that was all part of it. But in the end, we had to build something that was worth building. It was only worth building if someone was willing to buy it, if someone was willing to use it in their everyday business, in their everyday lives.

When I joined Inktomi, we had that already with Search. Thousands and then millions of people were using our search every day. Would Traffic Server be even bigger? Would people pay for it? Use it in the core of their businesses? Would it make the fabric of the internet different and better? In the end I believe it did.

You then start to wonder, what will my stock be worth? Could it be worth a million dollars? What if my stock was worth a million dollars? How would that change my life? I saw my small house that was loved and livable but kind of a joke among my relatives because it was so tiny.

The house we left behind in Pittsburgh had nine fireplaces, two kitchens, and a granite turret with stained glass windows. When we bought that house we imagined our daughter snuggling up in the granite turret reading books while it snowed outside. Our California house was a 1,600 square foot rancher with three bedrooms and a tiny office. It was in a great location; I could walk to work and easily walk home for lunch. Sure, the California house was worth twice that of the Pittsburgh place, but it was still kind of embarrassing that it was all we could afford.

My wife and I had not only downsized our house but also our lives in some ways. We moved away from our friends and family to join this adventure in California. We didn't have grandparents around to help us with our daughter. What if all these hours I was spending at work turned into nothing but a below market salary for a few years? All my wife's time spent alone raising a newborn would have been for nothing.

If the company went IPO, would I be able to buy a new house? I looked at my wife and new daughter. We had moved to California where we didn't know a soul. While I was off working long hours at Inktomi, my wife had to single-handedly take care of our daughter as she grew from a newborn into a toddler.

Maybe we could get a full time housekeeper and a nanny so my wife could have more free time. Our daughter was getting close to kindergarten age, we could put her into a great school, no matter the cost. I was working too much, ignoring my health, and not spending enough time with the family. More money could mean less work.

In Silicon Valley there is this idea of FU money—when you make enough money that you can tell your boss "fuck you." I actually liked the work, but how would it feel to be able to work the hours that I wanted? If I had FU money, I could relax a bit more and prioritize my time more in favor of myself and my family.

I could work out more. I could come home earlier from work. We could go on more family vacations. My wife had a passion for travel. We had spent our first anniversary backpacking around Europe. If we had more money, that could translate into more travel. She could indulge her passion for travel, and we could explore the world, maybe even travel first class and leave the backpacks behind.

Eventually the day came when we found out what that stock was really worth. The day of the IPO, June 11, 1998. The market set the IPO price at $18 per share. It ended the day around double that, $36 per share. Now this shit is real. It turns out Inktomi had the second most successful IPO of 1998. eBay was the first.[8] I thought it was crazy that a website that basically put yard sales online was worth more than Inktomi with all our advanced technology.

Regardless, on the day of the IPO, everyone with options now knows what they are worth. People are doing the math. They are setting up spreadsheets and following stock tickers. At the time of the IPO, we had around 250 people. On paper that day I would bet at least fifty of them were worth over $1 million. Eventually the two founders would be worth over a billion dollars each at the peak. These were not the normal trajectories of a successful academic careers. We had turned a bunch of research computer scientists into rich tech startup entrepreneurs.

It was a heady day at the office. We had one conference room setup with screens showing CNBC and running stock graphs

---

8   Ibid.

of INKT, our new stock symbol. There were water gun fights breaking out around the office, which was an Inktomi tradition from the early days. Using water guns around computers maybe wasn't the smartest thing, but it was certainly exciting. In the early days, the engineering teams fought each other: Search versus Traffic Server. Later it was Engineering versus Marketing.

It was a day to bask in the worth of what we had built and to start dreaming of what to do next. That day, some of us at Inktomi would go on to make multiple fortunes and create our own web of companies. Others would not make a cent off the stock options they had been granted but would nonetheless go on to successful careers. A few would even make enough to retire from Inktomi and never work again.

My friend John walked by the conference room where the stock ticker was projected up on the wall. The stock price was surreal. He did some math in his head and realized he could just walk out the door if he could have sold it all at that point. He took a break and went for a walk.

Our office in San Mateo was near the San Francisco Bay, with lovely paths along the estuaries. Walking along the waterways in the California sun, it didn't feel real, so he just went back to work. Somehow he felt like he owed our new investors the effort to make the price seem more reasonable, to justify it. If we kept working, we could make the company really worth what the stock market was telling us it was worth.

That day I had a regular one-to-one scheduled with my boss. He looked a little shell shocked. He was the guy who recruited me. He was the guy who made Traffic Server happen. He was a visionary, a genius, a slave driver, and a hard worker. He had been right. I remember asking him how it felt to be a millionaire. He looked embarrassed and said he wasn't a millionaire. This confused me. I had done my math; I had my spreadsheet. I knew the stock price and I knew how many shares I had. I knew that on paper I had crossed that mark. This guy was a millionaire for sure. Was he stupid? No. Was he being technical?

Sure he had stock that on paper was worth over a million. Probably many millions in his case. But it was just on paper. He couldn't sell that stock on that day. For these technical reasons, was he denying he was a millionaire? I don't know why he denied it.

For him, I think it had been about the challenge. About seeing if he could do it. Could he corral a bunch of us geek savants? Could he get us to make a thing that was worth something? Could we change the world? Maybe he was depressed that the challenge seemed to be over. The stock he had used as a tool to motivate us at times now had an explicit value.

But maybe in his mind he was above all that. Maybe it embarrassed him that he was worth so much money. If he was embarrassed by money, it would only get worse. Things were just starting to take off.

After the Inktomi IPO, there started to be two classes of employees, those who joined before the IPO and those who joined after. Before an IPO, a company is typically more generous with their stock because they need to hire people and want to conserve cash. After an IPO, the company will have cash on hand as a result of the IPO, so they will tend to pay higher salaries and offer smaller stock option grants. As a result of all this, folks who joined Inktomi before the IPO tended to have large stock grants worth quite a bit, a.k.a. millions of dollars.

The pre-IPO crowd started to spend their newfound wealth. The parking lot started filling up with BMWs and Porsches. Formerly chubby engineers started slimming down and dressing better as they hired personal trainers and got makeovers. I complimented one guy on his sweater, and he replied, "Thanks, I chose it because I thought it had the highest chance of making other people feel jealous."

Some guys even changed dramatically, getting plastic surgery and hair transplants. Trendy $100 haircuts started appearing on the heads of guys who used to look like they cut their own hair. Girlfriends and boyfriends were replaced. Spouses were upgraded. What had been a fairly homogeneous group of people started to bifurcate into the well off and the truly wealthy.

There was talk behind closed doors advising us in the pre-IPO group to be more sensitive. The company had to keep growing and hiring. We didn't want the newer employees to feel bad. It was great that you had your new spending power but try not to brag about it. I remember one of our more recent hires back then asking me how it felt to be a millionaire.

I tried to shrug it off saying, "What am I going to spend it on, some new socks? I already have enough socks." At the ten-year anniversary party for Inktomi, he told me he remembered me saying that, thinking I was quite humble. In fact, at the time I was selling Inktomi stock to buy my family that new house. It felt great, and a little bit scary.

In the end, money changed my perspective in a big way. It changed all of us at Inktomi. It would be a lie to say the money hurt us. It kept us going as a company. It helped us provide jobs for new employees. It bought my family a new house, our kids a good education. It provided the essentials, but also countless other luxuries. That said, I have plenty of socks.

I don't think I'll ever have that same feeling of working on clever ideas that will change the world. Steve Jobs talked about making a dent in the universe. At Inktomi we made our dent in the universe. Our techniques for lassoing together a bunch of computers to scale a website or search engine are standard practice today at Google and Facebook. Our proxy cache architecture for organizing and moving data around the internet is common practice for almost all websites, and providing these services is a part of what cloud computing companies like Amazon provide today.

I'll never feel the same way as I did when we were running around the office with water guns as our stock skyrocketed. But I suppose that is part of life. Money, too, is a part of life. And from then on out, it would change us and allow us to take more risks in the future. Some that would pay off and more than a few that would tank.

CHAPTER 7

HABANERO BURGER

———

Prince of Wales Pub, August 1999

San Mateo, California

After the first bite, my mouth exploded. My eyes began watering. This was the spiciest burger I had ever eaten. The bartender warned me, even made me sign a waiver before he would pass over the famous habanero burger. My co-workers all laughed and cheered me on as I continued to chew. My challenge was to eat the entire habanero burger. It was now a part of our tradition for new hires at Inktomi.

I wasn't a new hire, but I didn't want to be left out. Inktomi had moved into new offices near the Prince of Wales pub in San Mateo, so for some reason it was decided that everyone on the team should take the challenge. It was good for team bonding. Soon "I survived the Habanero Burger" bumper stickers started showing up in cubicles around the office. I survived mine and thus earned the right to cheer others on as they took the same challenge.

The Prince of Wales Pub was a hole in the wall bar in San Mateo. It was dark and dingy and effected that British Pub feel. Lots of British beers on tap and even more in the bottle. Of course, being in California, their pub food had a more American slant to it. One of the more unique items on the menu was the habanero burger. This was a burger with a slathering of habanero paste on top of the burger. It was crazy spicy.

By this time Inktomi had been a public company for about a year. We were growing like crazy and hiring lots of new folks. We were looking for ways to make the new people feel like part of the team. Adding a silly tradition like spicy burger eating seemed like a good way to do this. It let us gather outside of the office and get to know our ever-expanding team on a more personal level.

If you ate one of the burgers, they would put your name on the wall. Eventually the wall got full, so they started putting people's names on a website.[9] (Yes, they even listed your email address, something you would never do today.) Eating that burger would end up changing my career. Silicon Valley in the early 2000s was in a frenzy. There were not enough people to work at all the startups. Companies were going public all too often and raising insane amounts of money. They needed to hire people to make those startups work.

Recruiters were key to this process. Companies would hire recruiters to help them find employees. Typically, recruiters got some fraction of the new employee's salary. A talented

---

9   The Habanero Hamburger "Hall of Flame", June 8th, 2002.

software engineer in 2000 would easily make over $100,000 per year in Silicon Valley. A recruiter placing a few software engineers per month could make many times that. Most software engineers are pretty introverted and not particularly good negotiators. They aren't good at looking for jobs. Recruiters help bridge this gap.

In 2000 Inktomi was flying high. We were in the business news on a regular basis. We had been around for a while, so early employees like me had vested most of our stock, which meant that our golden handcuffs were expiring. For a recruiter, it became a great fishing hole for new talent. Katya was a top recruiter and she specialized in high-end talent, folks with PhDs and experience with startups were her specialty. Lucky for her, I had eaten a habanero burger and lived to tell the tale. She found me on the Prince of Wales website and made a cold call to me at the office one day. I'm sure she had tried all the Inktomi folks on the Habanero Burger site. With me, she got a bite.

It turns out I was pretty unhappy at work. The company was growing at an insane pace and it didn't feel like a special place anymore. As the company grew, they added another layer of managers and I had a new director over me whom I didn't particularly like. It went from being a fun place to work, to a place obsessed with money and stock prices. I'm sure it's a tough position for a new director to be brought in to oversee a bunch of folks who had built the company and who had more money than they knew what to do with.

I had my "fuck you" money. I wasn't happy but I still had a lot of stock to vest. While walking home from work one day,

I calculated how much money I was making as my stock vested monthly. It was a lot. It was too much to walk away from at that point. The golden handcuffs were still in place. But I was working long hours and not taking care of myself or my family. I knew something had to change.

My new boss gave me some negative feedback in a review, and I was pissed about it. He could tell I was upset, he told me I could always quit. Thinking back about it now, maybe he was trying to push me out for some reason. I think I said something like "I don't need this," referring to the job. He called me on it. "Do you really have enough money that you don't need this job?" I thought about it and the answer was yes. I didn't need the job anymore. I just didn't want to quit and leave all my unvested stock behind though. Money was money. I would find another solution.

As Inktomi grew, they eventually added a Professional Services division. This was basically a consulting arm. We would charge people to help them customize our software for use in their networks. Gordon Heinrich was the new VP of Professional Services. He needed help and I decided to jump over from Product Development to Professional Services. I went where I was wanted. I had been one of the key engineers on the TS team. They were glad to have me.

The hours were easier, and I got to travel more on the company dime. When one of my friends heard about my move, he called it my "rest and vest" program. He was right. I was burned out. I had gained fifty pounds, and I was disgusted with myself. It was time to refocus, get in shape, and try something new. Lucky for me, I was able to move into PS where the hours were more reasonable, and I was a star player again.

As a key TS engineer, I had been on sales calls before. These are usually fun meetings. The sales guys have a big expense account, so they can woo the customer. You get to go out to nice meals and stay in nice hotels. The sales team talks up all the great things our product does. They have you there for backup should any technical questions come up. Often you're there to help show the customer that we're smarter than they are, and they need our stuff.

There is tension between sales and engineering. Sales likes to promise anything to make a sale. Engineering has to build a product that delivers. This is where PS comes in. If the customer likes the product but wants it customized, then they can hire Professional Services to make the customizations work.

In PS you're working for the customer as a consultant. Which generally means you're billing hours. This is very different from engineering where you're trying to release a product on a schedule. If it takes you eighty hours per week to get the product done, then you work eighty hours per week. In PS if you bill thirty hours per week, you're a hero.

One of our customers was Enron. Yeah, those guys. At the time they were revolutionizing the energy trading business. They decided to get into the internet business and dreamed up the *Enron Intelligent Network*. If you could trade energy, why not trade bandwidth? The theory was if you traded a commodity, it would make the market for that commodity more efficient and everyone would benefit. The problem with Enron's energy trading was that it was crooked; they were manipulating the energy markets, resulting in rolling blackouts in California.

Since Traffic Server could sit in a network and make it more efficient, it could also control the bandwidth that flowed through it. In theory this made sense. For Inktomi it was a win/win. We could sell TS to Enron, so they could have a tool to control bandwidth. We could also sell them a big Professional Services contract, so we could help them customize TS to help them realize their bandwidth trading dreams.

They called it BOS, bandwidth operating system, and it was part of EIN, the Enron Intelligent Network. It turns out this work would eventually lead me to meet Eric Holder, the US Attorney General under Obama. But that's another story.

During my "rest and vest" period, the Inktomi stock continued to slide. Eventually my unvested shares weren't worth enough to be much of an anchor. In those days we had lots of cold calls coming in. The building was filled with internet millionaires, so you never knew who was calling.

One day I got a cold call from Katya Allen. She was a cheery independent recruiter. Somehow we started talking, and she correctly deduced I wasn't too happy at Inktomi anymore. Over the years she placed me at three different companies, Centrata, Oracle, and Macrovision. I lasted three weeks at Centrata, a year at Oracle, and three months at Macrovision.

Centrata just seemed like a dysfunctional group of people, and even after a few weeks, I couldn't figure out what they were trying to do, so I left. Oracle was my first real experience working for a big company, I was a tiny cog in the huge machine. I found the pace to be glacial and the culture to be stifling. I did learn a lot about databases, which turned out to be very useful at my later startups.

Macrovision was a dying company. Their main product was copy protection for video tapes, so they were trying to build an internet product for battling peer-to-peer sharing. It was an interesting technical challenge, but the team was a disaster. They had some A players, but the C players were starting to take over. There is a saying, A players hire A players, B players hire C players. This team was getting diluted with C players.

Luckily Tim Tuttle came along and convinced me to cofound Truveo with him. It was a good excuse to leave the building. Truveo would be my biggest hit yet.

CHAPTER 8

PAPER MILLIONAIRE

───

1st Quarter 2000

San Mateo, California and Herndon, Virginia

It was probably a Thursday. For some reason we always seem to talk on Thursdays.

"I made it," he said.

"Huh?"

"At today's stock price, I made it," he reiterated. "I'm a millionaire."

Inktomi stock was testing new highs. Peter had joined shortly before the IPO, so he had pre-IPO shares. Something every aspiring techie in Silicon Valley wants to get their hands on. The key to stock options is starting with a low price and selling when the price goes up. When a company goes IPO the shares almost always go up.

By joining pre-IPO you're pretty much guaranteed that your options will be worth something. Inktomi was no exception, our shares doubled the day of the IPO. Two years later they were up over fifty times, from $18 to almost $1,000 split adjusted. In the run up to the IPO, Inktomi used options as a magic currency to hire a bunch of top tech talent.

Peter was one of those guys. He was also a polymath. We were roommates our senior year at Emory. While I was putzing around getting one degree, he got a combined BS/MS in Math and Computer Science and a BA in Russian. In the Spring of our senior year, recruiters from three-letter government agencies used to call our house asking for him. They called way too early in the morning. Peter was not an early riser. In the end he opted for a small company doing satellite data communications. He was on his way to becoming a top network software engineer.

Over a decade later, I was working at Inktomi in California. Peter was married and living in DC. This was lucky for Inktomi because AOL wanted a crack engineer in-house who could handle any problems the Inktomi software might cause when they dropped it into their network. Peter was the guy; it was a win/win. He ended up being an Inktomi employee, but he worked out of the AOL offices in Dulles, so he didn't have to displace his young family.

AOL was such an important customer, Inktomi had a small cadre of folks there to make sure they were happy. Peter was the only one at AOL who had access to the source code to Traffic Server. If needed, he could fix bugs, recompile, and redeploy the software. This gave AOL peace of mind, if not direct access to our source code. It was a good example of how small companies can work around the concerns of larger ones.

One other trick about stock option grants is they vest over time. This means you don't get all that stock at once. If that was the case you might just sell it and quit when the stock was worth something. The point of a stock option grant is to give you some skin in the game so you'll work hard, but also to keep you around for a while, and thus the vesting schedule. It's a form of golden handcuffs.

At Inktomi the vesting schedule was 2 percent per month with a six month cliff. This meant if you left before your six months you got no stock. At six months you got 12 percent and each month after that an additional 2 percent of your stock vests. When it vests, that means you can sell it. When Peter hit that million dollar mark, he was talking about the value of his stock grant, not what was vested or what he had sold. It was what he was worth on paper. He was a paper millionaire.

What would you do if you have a stock that had gone from $10 to $1,000 over the last two years? The trajectory at that point just keeps going up and to the right. You don't see a crash coming. Everyone around you is working their asses off to keep it going up. Everyone around you is optimistic it's going to keep going.

Also, as an employee, you can't sell the stock anytime you want. The SEC has rules about when employees can sell.

There are blackout days when employees can't sell. Those are usually around the end of the quarter when earnings are announced. Plus, if you sold, you would have to pay a ton of tax on the sale. It's always gone up, so it will probably keep going up, right? Why not wait to sell when it goes up even more?

Peter was embedded at AOL, surrounded by their engineering team. Being software geeks they had built scripts (programs) to keep track of their newfound wealth; the AOL guys all had scripts that looked up their stock values and texted them when significant milestone amounts were crossed, their stock split, etc. Remember, this is long before the iPhone came out. Peter's was a little more subtle. His script just logged and calculated the total each day and sent him a graph once a week. It was a heady environment, and however much his options were worth, it generally paled when compared to what the AOL guys had.

It wasn't just the original option grant. At Inktomi we were allowed to contribute a large amount to purchasing ESPP (Employee Stock Purchase Plan) shares, and everyone was doing it. And every year employees often got more options as part of their annual review. This is key to keeping employees from jumping ship to another company. Companies like Google and Facebook continue similar strategies today as a way of retaining their highly-skilled workforce. Option prices are set at the current market price for the stock, so for Peter the new option grants were way higher than the first batch, but it all added to the bottom line. His script had to get more complicated to account for different stock grants, ESPP, splits, etc.

All of those things kept you there and working hard and excited to keep going. Then there were thoughts of how to maximize the gain. If he exercised his options, he could start the long-term capital gains clock and pay less tax when he eventually sold them. Assuming they were worth more than he paid for them.

Peter shared an office at AOL for a while with the onsite engineer from Bay Networks. The guy was very bitter about the whole environment. Either he didn't get a bunch of options from Bay Networks, or they weren't appreciating like everyone else's. At any rate, his attitude got worse and worse by the day. He kept talking about going to work at a startup somewhere so he could get his share. Eventually he was gone. Like a hunter disappearing into the jungle, he was off in search of bigger game.

So unlike most of the people Peter was working with at the time, he never sold any of his options or shares. Other people bought expensive cars, houses, boats that they could only afford if their options kept appreciating. He was never interested in any of that. He couldn't imagine driving to work in a Ferrari, really. The Ferrari and Lamborghini dealerships are still just down the street from the AOL office today. He was more content to think his future was set. He considered selling enough of it to pay off the house, but that seemed foolish since the value of the shares that he sold would be so much higher if he waited.

The press Inktomi got was great. In an article covering top tech stocks to watch for the long term, the lead photo in the article had a picture of our CEO, Dave Peterschmidt standing with his hands on his hips looking like he owned the world. It was pretty convincing. Peter had never been on a ride like that before, and it seemed impossible the stock would ever go down significantly. Everyone was so enthusiastic about the company and the business that he never saw the downfall coming.

We were, of course, changing the way that the world did things, so how could that end? And it was true that we changed the world. It's hard to watch a movie now that was filmed before 2000 and not think at some point *Wouldn't it be easier if the character just looked this up on the internet?* or *Just call his cell phone!*

Ah, but then it starts going down. Is this just a dip or a trend? The internet is growing like mad, it's part of everyday life for more and more people. Surely it's here to stay. Surely Inktomi is an integral part of that, so it will come back. Surely Inktomi customers will keep growing and paying Inktomi and things will get back to normal.

Peter got another stock grant in April of 2000. He remembers it because he was on vacation in St. Croix at the time, and his wife Susan was pregnant. He had his review over the phone, and when his manager told him the grant price on his new options, he was thrilled. It was about $60 less than he thought the stock was going for (he hadn't been following his script because he was on vacation). The stock had dropped so much that week that the new options looked cheap. "This will be great when the stock went back up and split again," he mentioned to his wife, rejoining her poolside where she was enjoying her virgin Pina Colada. Of course it was the beginning of the end.

Then it continues going down, and you remember when your stock was worth $1 million. If you sell now, then you won't get back to that number. Maybe better to hold on and hope it comes back. Then it drops more, and you think, *Wow, that's low. I wouldn't want to sell at that price, it's almost not worth it.* A few months later and the stock is even lower. Now you think, *Well shit, it's not even worth selling now. Let's just let it ride and see where it goes.* And thus you ride the price down to nothing. Eventually the stock is worth less than your option price, and really not worth anything.

As this is happening, Inktomi is struggling to figure out where its business went. How do they keep key employees to make the business work? What businesses do they keep? What employees do they keep? It's a grueling phase to go through. The company can reprice options on grants that are now underwater, but that doesn't help if the stock keeps going down. In the end, Yahoo! bought Inktomi for $1.63 per share, split adjusted. That was about a third of the price of the stock on IPO day, five years earlier.

In retrospect Peter should have called his broker instead of me. He should have sold all his stock options that day when it hit it's all time high. But you can never predict these things. At the time you don't know it will be the all-time high. It's just the high so far, which you've been seeing repeatedly for the last two years.

So what's a better approach? A conservative approach is sell as you vest. This means each month when you vest your 2 percent of your grant, sell it. It's a corollary to dollar cost averaging. In the case of Inktomi, it means he would have left a lot of money on the table as the stock went up, but he would have preserved a lot of wealth by selling as the stock went down.

"I can't say that I have any great regrets though. I worked really hard in the Inktomi days but felt like I was appreciated for it. It was my favorite job of my career, stock options notwithstanding," he told me. "Would have been nice to have cashed some of that in though."

When Yahoo! bought Inktomi his ESPP shares were cashed out at that $1.63. At least he had capital loss deductions to spread over the next ten years or so.

In the end, AOL hired Peter where he continues to work on networking software. Yahoo! open sourced the Traffic Server source code, and it's still in wide use today, making the internet a better place. Former powerhouses of the internet, Yahoo! and AOL are now part of Verizon.

3

TRUVEO DAYS

CHAPTER 9

RED SWOOSH

"Dude you kill me with that circular buffer shit!" Bowman giggled after we jumped into his convertible Mercedes SL500. We had just pitched yet another venture capitalist on how Red Swoosh was going to take the world by storm. Bowman was one of those bigger than life characters. He had been early at Exodus and made a "shit ton" of money there. He would complain that the ATMs wouldn't give out $50 bills, so his wallet was stuffed with crappy $20s if he couldn't find his favorite ATM in Palo Alto, or God forbid, it was out of $50s.

Exodus, like Inktomi, was in the internet infrastructure business. Exodus built the pipes. Inktomi built the servers. It was a match made in heaven and the markets had eaten it up, right until the very end. Red Swoosh was the brainchild of Travis Kalanick, who dropped out of UCLA to start Scour, a Napster competitor. Napster and Scour made it their business to help users share content, mainly music, mostly by violating copyright law. Red Swoosh was Kalanick's second go around, this time to build a legit business off the idea of P2P, or peer-to-peer.

Travis was the brilliant young founder and the VCs had brought Bowman and me in for some adult supervision. In retrospect it's funny that the VCs thought that we were better than Travis. Rob was a chain smoker and had some top end Mercedes that he drove fast and hard. He was on the verge of losing his license because of speeding tickets. But Rob was only slightly older than Travis, and I was thirty-nine. Maybe it's because we had had exits with Exodus and Inktomi.

Red Swoosh was providing a revolutionary Peer-to-Peer Content Delivery Network, or P2P CDN. This meant if you wanted to publish a big video game or software update, we could deliver those bits to your users much cheaper than other alternatives like Akamai who hosted the content on massive servers distributed around the internet. Basically Akamai would make copies in their servers, and when you decided to start your download, they would grab a copy from the nearest server.

The genius behind Red Swoosh is we would deliver your download from other PCs that had already downloaded it. In fact, we would split it up into little pieces, so we could grab a small bit from each of a thousand different PCs, almost simultaneously. The result was that your download happened blazingly fast but cost us almost nothing. We served the download by sharing the resources of potentially millions of other PCs. The PC owners didn't mind because the overhead on their PCs was minimal.

I was the new Red Swoosh CTO (Chief Technology Officer), and I knew exactly how to move bits around the internet. At Inktomi this was our forté with Traffic Server. I liked the

P2P angle. P2P was all the rage back then. Travis figured out a business plan that leveraged P2P for content owners that wanted to deliver it cheaply and securely. Red Swoosh was getting paid to deliver these files, not helping users steal them. Frankly it was a pretty great idea.

The VC had asked the questions that VCs always ask. "What's your secret sauce?" came the predictable question.

"We have millions of nodes communicating over highly disparate network connections," I began. "In this case, we'll need to make sure to effectively utilize the CPU, memory, and the network resources. One key to our design is an adaptive data flow algorithm with circular buffers." At this point I got excited and started drawing lots of lines and circles on the whiteboard. I thought this was a cool idea, and I let my enthusiasm show through, careful not to drone on too long and bore them.

In fact the idea of adaptive dataflow and circular buffers is what we had used at Inktomi. My role was to answer the VCs' questions and wow them a bit with a lecture on internet data flow. Bowman thought they ate it up. The key with the VCs is to show them you know your stuff. You need to explain it in a way that makes sense but also take it a little further, so they are slightly confused and don't want to look stupid. You need to make sure they know that you know what you're doing.

After NeoPyx, my previous startup, imploded, I was looking for something new. I had learned it was difficult to raise money if you didn't have a hook. Sure I was early at Inktomi, and I had built some key technology there, led teams, worked with top customers like Microsoft, AOL, and Enron. But I hadn't shown the VCs that I could make things happen on my own.

At Red Swoosh we had some cool technology and some real customers, but it wasn't clear that folks would pay a lot of money for our product. One thing that swayed me was that we had a term sheet from August Capital for a $3 million round. A term sheet is an agreement where a VC agrees to put money into your startup based on various terms. In the case of Red Swoosh, the August Capital term sheet was contingent on a co-lead. That meant they would put in $5 million if we could find another VC who would put in $5 million. At the time I took this as a very positive sign.

Now that I'm more seasoned, I realize this is a mediocre commitment. Basically they think this might be worth something, so if the company can convince someone else that it's worth something, then they will come in on the round. It's like penciling in a date on your calendar. You'll keep it open as long as nothing better comes along. This also plays into the fear of looking stupid, and a hedge against not missing out (FOMO, fear of missing out). If someone else comes on board, this means it probably wasn't stupid. By having the term sheet out there, they are lending some credibility to the company, but they're not convinced enough to go all in and simply fund the entire round themselves.

I spent the summer of 2002 hanging around with the Red Swoosh team, mainly going to meetings with VCs and ripping all my CDs to mp3 files. It was the nuclear winter of Silicon Valley. The summer after 9/11 no one was really investing. People were still just going through the motions. August Capital was making a conservative and smart move. They saw potential in Red Swoosh, but it was not yet the time again for bold bets. The dot-com crash was still memorable. The post 9/11 future was still quite murky.

Rob realized that even with all my talk of circular buffers, the VCs were still not convinced. He had the idea to get some big wig to come in and do a technology review. If we could find someone who the VCs respected, we could spend some time showing him how good we were, and he could also vouch for us. It turns out that Amy Henley, our Director of Operations, was the daughter of Oracle's CFO, Jeff Henley.

"Amy, your dad is the freaking CFO over at Oracle. Ask him if he can get some big muckety muck there to come over here and take a look at what we're doing," said Bowman. "We need someone to talk some sense into these VCs."

I was surprised Amy's dad was the CFO at Oracle. Amy seemed shy and a little too granola to be the daughter of a rich, high powered Silicon Valley executive. What was she doing working at Red Swoosh anyway? In 2002, Oracle was one of the largest software companies in Silicon Valley.

That's how I ended up meeting Roger Bamford.

Bamford was about ten years older than I was. He had been very early at Oracle. Essentially he's the guy who wrote the database. The guy is a true Silicon Valley hero. Later when I worked at Oracle, I had access to the actual source code to the Oracle database. Sure enough, Roger's name was all over it.

We brought Roger by the Red Swoosh office on High Street in Palo Alto to spend some time with him. I gave him my circular buffer spiel. We talked about all the cool problems we had solved with our P2P system. How to make sure we didn't have rogue nodes joining in and corrupting data, how we protected and validated the content. It was a fun meeting. Rob pushed Roger to see if he could be a reference for us. Roger shrugged his shoulders and said, "Sure." I would later recognize this as a wholehearted yes for Roger, who is a pretty low key guy given his stature in the valley.

Rob's instincts were dead on, getting a senior figure like Roger on our side was a good strategy. Investing isn't just about the good idea, it's about the people, relationships, and trust. While it didn't help Red Swoosh, my relationship with Roger would impact my later startups as well as my personal life.

In the end, Rob and I left Red Swoosh. Travis scaled back the company and kept going. He had some revenue, so he just kept a skeleton team around and rebuilt. He outlived the nuclear winter. Eventually Mark Cuban (yes, that Mark Cuban) came in as an angel investor. They were able to scale the business up and sell it to Akamai, where Travis became VP of P2P Content Delivery. Travis proved he had the smarts and tenacity for startup success.

Travis would later found Uber, making a huge impact on transportation and society. I can honestly say that I was a CTO under Travis Kalanick at his previous company.

In computer science there is a common bug called an "off by one" error. This is when your program miscalculates and is "off by one" where it seems like it shouldn't be. From a career standpoint maybe I made an off by one error here. But I was busy with Truveo, which turned out to be one of my greatest hits.

My Silicon Valley network was growing link by link. Bamford was one of our first angel investors at Truveo, giving us his classic shrug and saying sure, he would put some money in.

CHAPTER 10

TRUVEO BEGINS

———

"On my end, Bang Networks closed down last fall. Since then, I took a little time off and then spent most of my time researching a few projects. I am starting to sort out my next steps and would be interested in your feedback."

— TIM TUTTLE 2004, SAN FRANCISCO, CALIFORNIA

Truveo was a perfect storm of timing, talent, and technology. In some ways it was a case study of how to get a company off the ground and turn it into a successful exit.

BOOTSTRAP

To get started, you have to bootstrap somehow. You need to have the time and the funds to work on your idea. In Tim Tuttle's case, he had wrapped up his previous company and was able to live off his savings as he worked on ideas for his next company. I was working at Macrovision but didn't love the job, and I hated the commute. I hadn't made enough money from Inktomi that I could retire, but I could afford to live without a salary for a while. Thus when Tim approached me, I was ready and able to take some time off and try something new.

After 9/11 there was a freeze in startup funding. Some called it a nuclear winter. By 2004 the nuclear winter was over, and things were starting to move again. I was tired of working for large companies, so when Tim contacted me and said he was working on a new idea and wanted to get my input, I was ready.

I had tried my hand at three startups by then. The first one, Inktomi, was a smash hit. At the other two I had struggled to land financing and eventually gave up. Tim was a fellow techie; he had a PhD from MIT. But he was also a fundraising guru and more interested in the business side than I was. At his previous company he had raised over $10 million. I had built real products at scale during my time at Inktomi. My CS PhD and my affiliation with Carnegie Mellon University added shine to my resume. Together we were the perfect team.

THE IDEA

Tim's idea was to build a video search engine. In 2004 internet video was nascent. Netflix was shipping DVDs by mail, not streaming movies. YouTube did not yet exist. But these things were just around the corner. Comedy Central had started putting some of their top shows, like *The Daily Show with Jon Stewart*, streaming on the internet in high quality. Reuters had a news site with all their latest video news stories. MSN added video to their portal, to show off Microsoft's Windows Media technology.

Things were starting to happen. Tim noticed this trend. He also saw that this video was not showing up in Google or Yahoo! This was an opportunity. Search engines use data collected from crawling the web. Web crawlers are programs that are constantly scouring the internet looking for content to index. Why were Google's crawlers not finding all this great video that was starting to show up?

It turns out, crawling for video is a hard problem. There are a few reasons for this. Video content owners are worried about piracy. They don't want to make it easy to download their videos and share them on BitTorrent or other P2P networks. Content owners want to control their video content. They want viewers to watch the video by streaming it from their website, where they can serve ads or charge subscription fees to make money off the viewers.

These new video sites were designed using what was at the time new technology, mainly browser side technology, called AJAX (asynchronous JavaScript and XML). When you surf the web, the web browser grabs content from a server and formats it for you. In the early days, web content was static. In 2004, things started to change dramatically. Web browsers were getting more sophisticated. Today we don't think anything of clicking and dragging on a map embedded in a webpage. But in 2005, Google maps came out with this ability, and it was like magic.

Browsers were becoming smart. They turned from simple display programs to compute engines that could run almost any code. The new video rich websites that began showing up in 2004 leveraged this idea of client side controls. This meant the browser was now integral in rendering and controlling video served from a website. Because of this change, search engines were essentially blind to this new kind of content. Tim realized this and was starting to build a new kind of crawler that could find video on the internet, something Google and Yahoo! could not do in 2004. This was an opportunity.

THE RIGHT BACKGROUND

Back at Inktomi I led a project to build a streaming media cache. In the late '90s streaming media was still very niche, but it took a lot of bandwidth, which made caching a perfect solution. At Inktomi we realized by caching this content in servers embedded in the network, we could greatly improve the end user experience and cut down the expensive bandwidth costs of serving video (and audio). The dot-com crash happened before our streaming media cache got wide use, but it taught me a lot about the technicalities of serving video over the internet.

By 2004, I was still fascinated by the minutia of internet video. I was trying to build a system to find video and reformat it for my fancy new $10,000 plasma TV. My day job was actually building an anti-piracy product that Macrovision was hoping to sell to the movie studios.

Macrovision made its money by selling a copy protection system for video tapes. If you used a VCR in the '80s or '90s, you used Macrovision technology. The movie industry had persuaded Congress to pass a law requiring Macrovision technology in every VCR sold in America.

It was a good business while it lasted. In a post-Napster world, Macrovision's monopoly on video tape technology didn't mean a lot. They needed new ways to make money and leverage their existing business relationships, so they came up with the idea to provide copy protection that worked for P2P networks. In 2004 (and still today) you can download movies, music, and software off peer-to-peer networks where illegal copies are being served. This is the Napster problem.

Once someone has a copy of a movie, they can share it on a P2P network, and there isn't much the copyright holder can do about it. However, it turns out there are some things you can do to interfere with the downloads of P2P content. Macrovision started Project Hawkeye. The idea was to watch the P2P networks for content that Hollywood cared about. If we spotted a copy, then we would fire up our system to inter-fere with the downloads of those files. It was an interesting technical challenge. You had to identify movies or music even though the copies weren't perfect. Once you identified a copy on the network, you had to figure out a way to keep people from downloading it.

P2P networks are built on the idea of cooperation. If I have a copy I want to share, I let other users on the network connect to my computer and share it. So one strategy we had was to pretend we had copies, so users would connect to us, but we wouldn't share legitimate copies. Basically my job was to help reverse engineer these P2P networks and come up with ways to thwart them, but only for content our customers wanted to protect. P2P networks aren't illegal per se, so we didn't want to entirely disrupt them. You could be sharing something legitimate, say a copy of the US Constitution, and that would be totally fine.

My experience in building internet video related products at Inktomi, and later Macrovision, was a perfect fit for Tim's new idea for a startup.

IT'S ALL ABOUT THE TEAM

When investors evaluate an early stage company, they first look at the team. Are these people smart? Are they determined? Can they actually build the technology that they are proposing? Are they connected with other high quality folks, so they can build out the rest of the team? Tim and I had proven ourselves at our previous companies, Bang Networks and Inktomi. Our backgrounds checked all these boxes.

COLLABORATING

At first we were meeting on a weekly basis. Tim lived in the Mission District of San Francisco. This is right around the time that medicinal marijuana became legal in California, and there was a dispensary across the street from his place, which added to the sketchy feel of the neighborhood. I lived in San Carlos, about a forty-minute drive down the peninsula from San Francisco. We were in suburbia with our fancy house that Inktomi bought. It was exciting to drive up to the city for our weekly meetings, even though I was a bit worried about parking my BMW 740i in his neighborhood. Occasionally, we would meet at our place. Tim was on an ultimate frisbee team at Stanford, a few exits from our house, which made things convenient.

THE PITCH

In the early days, we worked on the pitch and the prototype mostly. Tim put together the PowerPoint and we would practice giving the pitch to an empty room. Practicing the pitch is critical. It's really like a piece of performance art. You must treat it this way. You don't want to fumble; you need to sound confident and smooth. You need to ensure you hit the critical points and excite the investors. Mostly, Tim did the presentation, and I had a few slides on technology. Tim was the CEO and I was the CTO, so this made sense.

SHOWTIME

Once you have the deck and have practiced it to perfection, then it's showtime. You need to line up meetings where you can give the pitch. In Silicon Valley this is as likely to be a coffee shop as it is a meeting room at a venture capital firm. You have to start with your network. Who do you know that can give you good advice? Who can connect you to other potential investors? It's critical to **ask for advice, not money.** Especially in the early meetings. You haven't tested your pitch yet. Your thesis is untested on investors. It's best to try some slightly friendly folks as your initial audience. Remember, this is theater. Your first few presentations are like a dress rehearsal. You want to rapidly iterate on your pitch, just as you will later about your product.

One of our first meetings was with Eric Brewer. Eric was a founder of Inktomi and a well-respected Computer Science Professor at Berkeley. We made the trek across the Bay Bridge to meet with Eric at his university office. It brought back good memories of the early days at Inktomi. Eric got the technology and the idea. He wasn't investing, but he could be a reference for us. I admit I was a little disappointed that he didn't offer to invest right then. But that would be too easy. He saw how our technology was unique, and how it could be the basis for a business. Having someone like Eric, a Berkeley Computer Science Professor and successful internet startup founder, say you had a good idea, was worth more than money.

RULES AND DEBRIEF

A startup pitch has some rules. The pitch should be concise and well-practiced. Each founder should have at least a few slides to make sure the investor gets a chance to hear from both and get a feel for them. He is evaluating the people as well as the idea.

Founders should not argue during the meeting. You need to present a unified front. Even if one founder says something you disagree with, don't contradict each other or cut each other down. It's your time to show that you're a good team and can work together. You can have healthy disagreements, but they should show you're considering all sides of an issue, not just arguing. Take notes during the pitch, so you can discuss any disagreements *after* the pitch is over and the investor has left the room.

It's critical to debrief after each session. Think about what worked and what didn't. You will find that investors tend to ask the same questions over and over. If there is a question that stumped the investor, you take note. Come up with a good answer. It's likely you'll get the same question on a future pitch. Test your new answer next time. Remember, this is like theater. Your presentation should get better each time you do it. The more you present and the more you hone your pitch, the better it will become over time. After you've done this a few times, you'll have great answers to all the investors' questions. You'll sound like a genius who really knows your shit. This is your goal.

Also take note of people or companies the investors mention. Really, this is the crux of the advice he can give you. Does he know of people who like to invest in your business or technology area? Does he know of other companies that are doing similar things to what you're doing?

When we were pitching Truveo, Google was making noise about something that sounded similar. Investors were warning us that Google would kill us. As you can imagine, the first time we heard this we didn't have a great answer.

We dug around and found that Google was doing something called GoogleTV at the time. They were indexing the closed captioning of broadcast TV. This was interesting, but it wasn't competitive at all. The next time we got this comment, we had a good response.

"Yes, we know. Google is working on indexing the closed captioning of TV shows. This is an interesting research project but not competitive with what we're doing," we would say confidently. "We're finding video content on the web that Google doesn't have in its index. The GoogleTV project just shows that video is important and the space is heating up."

Think of the pitching as an iterative process. Try to learn something from each meeting. Treat it as a discovery project. You truly want to get advice from the investors. Who else do they know that might be interested in your project? Use your network to expand your net of potential investors. At some point, they will ask how much money you're raising, and they will want to get into the details around that. It gives you the opportunity to ask if they know someone who might be interested in investing. If you're lucky, they will.

"Do you know of anyone who might be interested in investing?" you ask.

"Me!" is what you hope they respond.

BE CAREFUL, BE CAGEY

As you start talking about who is investing and at what valuation, you need to be careful. Remember, you're trying to sell a product and negotiate a price. The investment in your company is really a purchase. The price depends on the demand. You need to make a market for your stock. You want investors excited. Besides getting them excited about your team and tech, you also need to let them know other investors are interested, maybe so much that no one else can invest. People always want what they can't have.

"We're raising a million, and right now it looks like we're over-subscribed." This lets them know that you don't need their money. If you indicate they might not be able to invest, then they will likely start *selling you* on why they should invest.

FOMO, Fear Of Missing Out, is real and it works. It allows you to generate more interest in your company and find the investors that can help you most. If you can take money from someone who has valuable industry connections or experience building products in a similar area, this investor should win out over simple "dumb money." Of course, smarter money may come at a higher price. Terms from a well-known investor may not be as good as terms from a less sophisticated investor. But your goals should be to make a market for your stock. The more investors interested, the better chances you have of getting a good price.

"Who else is investing?" is a question you'll get asked. Investors are like lemmings. If someone they know and respect is investing, they will want to invest as well. Be careful how you answer this question. If you have a committed champion, then you may want to mention his or her name. But if the person you mention is a sophisticated investor, this could lead to investors colluding and driving down your valuation.

For example, let's say you're having conversations with two investors, they are both interested and willing to lead your round. Ideally, you want to play them off each other. If Investor A gives you a valuation of $8 million and Investor B gives you a $9 million valuation, you can go back to Investor A and say, "I really like you and think you would be a good fit for us, but I'm getting terms for a $9 million valuation already, and I need to think about what's best for the company."

At this point Investor A will want to know as much as possible about Investor B. Don't connect them. Don't mention their names to each other. It's much better for them to use their imaginations. You want them to compete, and the less they know about their competition, the better. If they do find out about each other, they may collude and push down your valuation. They may come back together and say, "We really like what you're doing, but we're only going to be able to offer you a $7 million valuation."

Information is power. Be careful what you share.

Of course in the beginning you won't have any investors, so what do you say? You don't want to lie, but you also need to say something positive. Something like, "We're in talks with a number of highly respected individuals," could work, but make sure it's true. At the start, you want to set up a lot of meetings at once. Mine your network and fill up your calendar. Meetings should beget meetings. As you meet investors, hopefully they will introduce you to more investors.

Again, *ask for advice*. When someone is asked for advice, they are implicitly on your side. You're saying, "Hey I'm working on this project and I would like your advice." They will want to help. If you ask for money, then they start thinking about why they should or shouldn't invest. If someone is a qualified investor and you ask for their advice, they may offer to invest. But that's not the way to start the conversation.

THE BIG CHEESE

We followed this playbook at Truveo. We practiced our pitch; we filled our calendars, and we went out and made the rounds. As I mentioned, our first meeting was with Eric

Brewer. Later, we met with Vince Vannelli, whom Tim and I both knew from our previous companies. Vince was on the board of Tim's prior company, Bang Networks, and he had been an exec at Inktomi, my first startup.

Vince was one of those "larger than life" guys. He was tall and athletic. He played water polo when he was at Stanford. Inktomi was a big win for Vince, and in 2004, he was starting his own venture capital firm, VSP Capital, and they were interested in hearing our pitch.

VSP had swanky offices in the San Francisco financial district. We met with Vince and gave him our pitch. It felt comfortable working with Vince, maybe because we had a history, and maybe because Vince is great at sales.

"I spoke to Brewer," Vince told us. My heart rate spiked. It seemed like we had a good meeting with Eric Brewer, but he wasn't investing. Was Vince going to tell us the same thing?

Tim and I nodded, waiting for him to continue, not wanting to give anything away.

"He said you guys seem to be onto something," Vince went on. We breathed a sigh of relief. In this case, collusion between potential investors worked in our favor.

"I want you to meet my partner Joann. She's a marketing guru. Since you're going to focus on direct-to-consumer marketing, she would be great to have on your side," he continued. Now he was starting to sell us on the advantages of taking money from his firm. This was a good sign.

In the end, Vince decided to lead our round and we negotiated a term sheet. VSP would invest the majority of the funds, but we needed to find additional investors to fill out the round. With a term sheet in hand, we continued our search for additional investors.

LESSONS

- Find a team that has the right skills and motivation.
- Build a prototype so you can demonstrate it to angels.
- Meet on a regular basis.
- Practice your pitch.
- Ask for advice, not money.
- Have lots of investor meetings.
- Talk to other founders, especially those who have raised capital.
- Debrief after each pitch:
  - What questions stumped you?
  - What answers seemed to work well?
  - Who did they say they could connect you with?
    - Make sure to follow up.
  - What other competitors did they bring up?
    - Research these and make sure you have positioning.
  - What concerns did they have?
    - See if you can better address those next time.
- Be careful with information, be cagey.

CHAPTER 11

JIGSAW OFFICES

———

2004 Jigsaw HQ, San Mateo, California

"What the hell happened to the network?!"

Things were shaping up with Truveo. We were making progress on the funding and starting to build a real product. I quit my job at Macrovision so I could focus full time on Truveo. It became clear we needed an office. Tim lived in San Francisco, and I lived in San Carlos. Somewhere in the middle would be ideal. It turned out one of my good friends, Jim Fowler, had just raised a second round for his company, Jigsaw, and they were moving into larger offices.

"Dude, we have plenty of space, you guys are more than welcome to use one of our offices," he offered. "Until we need it, of course," he added. Jigsaw was planning significant growth, and Fowler thought we would be able to hang out there for a month or so at least.

Fowler and I met when our sons became friends in preschool. He's truly a people person. He loves talking to people and getting their stories. This made him a great sales guy, and fun to be around. I was more on the introverted side of the scale, but Fowler drew me out and we became good friends. He had seen me try my hand at a couple startups that tanked, and he was happy to lend his advice and a bit of his spare office space to help me out.

When you're doing a startup, it's a good idea to stay in touch with other startups. Jigsaw was further along on the growth path. They were on their second round of funding. We were just closing our first. They were sales focused; we were tech focused. But Fowler being Fowler, he also had his finger on the pulse of early stage Silicon Valley startups. He could be a further reference point for us. As we got valuations, we could compare them with what other startups were getting. As we made job offers, we could compare those to what others were paying for similar positions.

All companies have a personality. Jigsaw's was a mirror of Fowler. It was boisterous, loud, and outgoing. Near the office was a Trader Joe's grocery store, a ubiquitous Silicon Valley chain. Fowler had noticed the ships bell they have at the front of the store. Cashiers ring it to get help from other staffers. It's kind of kitchy and goes with TJs nautical theme. Fowler decided Jigsaw should have a bell that his sales guys could ring when they made a big sale. So, as we were hunkered down in the office trying to write code and build out our website, we would occasionally be shocked out of our concentration by a sales guy hooting and ringing a bell. The occasional distraction was worth it for free office space.

We tried to be good tenants, especially since we weren't paying any rent. One of my jobs at the time was running our crawlers. Crawlers are programs that surf the web and suck up all the information they can find. Crawlers need to be tuned so they don't impact the performance of the websites they are crawling. Generally this is easy to do. Since the web is huge, the crawler can simply spread its attention around, not concentrating on any one website. You tune the crawler so it doesn't revisit the same site too often. I didn't think too much about how the crawlers would impact the network at the Jigsaw offices. I was just running it on a single machine at the time.

One afternoon I was tuning the crawler and seeing how hard I could push it. A few minutes after I kicked off another crawl. I heard Fowler yell, "What the hell happened to the network? It's down AGAIN?"

The IT guy was in the office next to ours, and I heard Fowler stomp up to his door and continue to complain. I was concentrating on some code I was writing, but at the edge of my consciousness, I was paying attention to the conversation.

"The network is up and running fine, I've been monitoring it since you started noticing issues, but I don't see any problems," the IT guy said.

Then it clicked. My crawlers were sucking up all the bandwidth for the entire office. The network wasn't going down. It was being overloaded by the Truveo crawlers. I popped open a window on my computer and killed the crawler and then sheepishly joined the conversation in the hall.

"Uh, sorry about that. I was running a crawler and apparently it got out of hand." I told them. The IT guy was relieved.

Fowler laughed. "Dude, you can't take down our network like that." He was still a little pissed, but relieved that at least we had figured out the problem.

"I'll add a bandwidth limiter to the code." I told them.

"Ok, you guys figure out the right solution," Fowler said delegating this problem to me and his IT guy as he walked back to his office. "Just make sure it doesn't happen again."

I made sure to keep my crawlers under control. A few months later, we found a small office in Burlingame that fit our needs. It was just in time; Jigsaw was expanding and Fowler notified us it was time to move on.

LESSONS
- Leverage your friend network.
- Take advantage of free office space.
- Don't forget to bandwidth limit your crawlers.

CHAPTER 12

HAWAII CODING

———

As we got more used to going on fancy vacations, we were turned on to the Grand Wailea Resort in Maui by Dennis McEvoy, my VP at Inktomi. Dennis was older and wealthier than we young crazies who were running around in the early days of the company. As we went through the IPO and started to realize what it was to have money, Dennis was a great resource. By this time we had two kids, and they were a handful. The Grand Wailea was a huge property, and it had its own private waterpark right on the beach. You could even join as a member and get special rates and bigger rooms.

Best of all, United had regular direct flights to Maui from SFO. Dennis mentioned you should fly First Class, because this way you would arrive well rested before going to lie by the pool while your kids spent time on the Tarzan rope swing. As to the cost difference for First versus Economy, at this point it just doesn't matter, he said. We eventually came around to his point of view.

After Inktomi, I went through a few other startups. My next big hit was a company called Truveo. At Truveo we were building a video search engine. I was the CTO and co-founder. In the first year, we worked on our own dime and got a prototype up and working. By the end of 2004, we had raised $1 million to fund our idea for a better video search engine. At this time, video was just starting to show up on the internet but was before YouTube. It was about the time Comedy Central started to put high quality video on its website. You could watch *The Daily Show with Jon Stewart* on their website, but you couldn't find his monologue in Google. We saw that as an opportunity.

For February Break, we were planning our regular pilgrimage to the Grand Wailea. Our kids were in the international school in Palo Alto, which meant we had an entire week off in February. We also had a good set of friends who were also parents at the school and liked to travel. As a bonus, that week in February is off season because most schools are in session and most regular people are working.

We had a group of three families. I was the only one doing startups. The other parents worked for big companies or banks. The international school was like this. You had a lot of interesting international folks, but many of them worked for big companies paying them to come from Italy or France to work in California. They liked the high-paying lifestyle, but they weren't risk takers. Their endgame was to work at IBM or HP and retire on a good pension. But in the meantime they made big money, and they weren't too opposed to spending it occasionally.

At the time, Truveo was a scrappy startup with a handful of employees, and I was the CTO. I had a conversation with my co-founder where I told him I would be working on this trip. He was skeptical but I assured him I could do it. He was right to be skeptical. I had already had an exit with Inktomi, and I was probably a little soft because of that. I had my big house, muni bond portfolio, kids in private school, and my Grand Wailea membership. He was a single guy with no family and still hungry for his exit.

So, on one hand I had my well-paid big company friends going out to the beach every day while I stayed back at the room writing code and running crawlers, programs that scour the internet, looking for video content to add to our search engine. On the other hand I had my co-founder back in chilly San Francisco plugging away on his task list as we marched toward the launch of our website. I'm sure my big company friends thought I was crazy. I was caught between these two worlds. I felt comfortable in both but not understood by either.

Each night at dinner we would discuss my progress. I was trying to get our video index up to a million videos. I love these friends, but they saw risk where I saw opportunity. Occasionally, the conversation would turn to them telling me they just didn't see how this company would succeed. I'm sure they thought they were helping me by giving me their honest opinions. Mainly it was just frustrating. There were times where I was sitting on the balcony of our room with my laptop and they would walk by below and shout up to me then walk away laughing and shaking their heads. They couldn't believe I was wasting my family vacation working.

My wife was very supportive. She knew what it was like to do startups, she was an entrepreneur from a young age. She had seen what had happened at Inktomi, and we had high hopes for Truveo. The dream was alive.

In the end it was worth it. Truveo had a very successful exit about a year later. We graduated from the Grand Wailea Hotel to the Grand Wailea Villas.

CHAPTER 13

DON'T DROP THAT DATA

2005 Burlingame, California

```
msql> drop database;   # be really careful
with this command
```

Samir Meghani walked into my office looking like he was about to cry.

"I fucked up," he said.

This was Friday morning; we were about to give Microsoft exclusive access to our search engine over the weekend. This was not the time for a fuckup.

"What happened?" I asked.

"I thought I was working with the test database, but I was on production. I dropped the database."

"You deleted our database." Deep breath. "Oh man," I said.

Thinking for a minute, trying not to go ballistic on him, I remembered we had just put in place our backup strategy. "Ok, well time to test our backups. Grab Pete and let's go through this together." Pete was our CTO and the guy who had insisted we put in place backup procedures and test them. Thank God for Pete.

In the end our backups were restored and some of the fresh crawler data re-loaded. The Microsoft trial went off without any issues. Well, a slight delay. They would eventually become a customer, but only two years later, after Truveo was acquired by AOL.

Samir was one of our first employees at Truveo. He grew up in Chicago and went to Illinois Math and Science Academy, one of the top high schools in the country. After that he studied Computer Science at MIT and was recruited to Oracle straight out of college. Oracle's a big company and not a lot of fun, but it's a great way to get introduced to Silicon Valley. Lucky for us, our post on an MIT alumni list got his attention.

Samir comes off as a fairly stoic and introverted guy at first. But once you get to know him, he's quite outgoing and entertaining.

When I interviewed him for the job at Truveo, I asked if he knows Linux.

"So, you know Linux pretty well?" I asked.

"Sure," said Samir. "I've been using it for a while."

"What's the command to tell how much disk space is left on the system?"

Pause. He looks down and seems to be examining his hands, folded on the table. "Ok, maybe I don't know it that well. I don't know every little arcane command," replied Samir.

"The command I was thinking of was DF, for display free disk. Seems I'm always running out of disk on our crawler machines, so I use that one a lot," I replied.

At Truveo, Samir was a hard worker and one of our first key employees. He came up to speed quickly and was always up for a technical challenge. After working for Truveo and then AOL after Truveo was acquired, Samir applied to Y Combinator (YC), and started his own company there. YC is Silicon Valley royalty. Being a YC alum has a special allure in the valley. Samir's YC company didn't have an exit, but now he was part of the *in crowd*; he's a YC founder.

Samir and I met recently at Zareen's in Palo Alto. We must be at peak Zareen's because you can't get a table there after 12:05 on a weekday. We arrive at 11:45 just as the crowd is building. For years I would buy Samir lunch every few weeks, and we would catch up. Now his latest startup had funding, so he was returning the favor.

"What do you think about all these engineers coming to Silicon Valley to get rich?" I asked.

"They're in for a disappointment. It's not the easy path to getting rich, but everyone thinks it is."

Samir had a front row seat to the Truveo acquisition, one of those once in a lifetime lottery ticket Silicon Valley wins. The company Tim and I co-founded went from nothing to an exit in two years, when AOL bought us just as internet video was becoming a thing. Everyone on our small team benefited, some would never need to work again, but that wouldn't stop us from trying.

Post-Truveo Samir has co-founded three more companies, one with me, which didn't go so well. The jury is still out on the latest one.

"I have friends that exclusively focused on getting rich after college," he said. "They decided to go the finance route, hedge funds and the like. They're rich now, and generally miserable." We agreed that money in and of itself isn't the key to a happy life. Sure, it helps, but when you focus exclusively on just the money, then you miss the fun of life.

Samir's measure of happiness is how many folks he consults about what he's working on each day. When you're working on a startup idea, that number is usually zero. It's just you and your ideas. These are the best times in many ways. It's like a writer staring at a blank page. So many possibilities. But is this really the way to get rich in Silicon Valley? Probably not, the odds are just so slim it's not really a good bet. But it's exciting and you can probably make a decent living at it once you learn how to play the game.

"The best way to get rich in Silicon Valley is to join a rocket ship. Join an Uber, Facebook, or Google before the IPO. Find the next hot startup and get in early. You'll make a decent salary and could get rich off the stock options." He's thought about this quite a bit.

So why isn't he doing this? He's on his fourth startup and the third one he's co-founded. He's not joining 100-person startups with lots of funding, he is creating new companies tabula rasa. I think it's for the joy of creating and the verification that comes with creating something new and useful. There is something satisfying about creating a new company and convincing people to get behind it. You start with an idea, then create a prototype and a slide deck. You pitch some investors, and if all goes well, you get some money from them. You then hire a few more people to help you out. You get a shitty little office of your own and you're off to the races. Even if it goes nowhere, which is what usually happens, you made something new happen. You created value. You made something that didn't exist before. You learned something, even in failure—especially in failure.

4

POST ECONOMIC DAYS

CHAPTER 14

CLUBHOUSE

———

The webcam on my iMac caught some strangers walking around our home office. This was 2007, before cheap internet connected security cameras, but there was software you could use to turn your webcam into a security camera of sorts. We were living in Vietnam and had left our California house empty. From halfway across the world, I logged into my Mac to see a video of a middle-aged couple wandering around my home office. These folks didn't look like burglars. Then I noticed they were accompanied by our real estate agent. Ah, yes! We had put our house on the market before we left. The camera had just caught our real estate agent giving a showing.

A few weeks later the Mac became unresponsive, and I wasn't able to log in anymore. Thus ended my first foray into video surveillance. It turns out this problem would bug me enough that I would start a company to try to solve it.

What do you do when you don't have to work anymore? For most people this is a dream. I've been confounded by this problem many times throughout my life. When I was in college and thinking about what I wanted to do with my life, the idea of working, and specifically working for someone else, bothered me. For a while, I would tell my friends in college I wanted to live on a subsistence farm. I liked the idea of not needing to worry about relying on other people to approve my lifestyle or what I was doing. This really confounded the pre-med and pre-law students I seemed to be surrounded by.

I ended up learning to code and to build things with code and around code. In a way, coding and startups are similar to subsistence farming. If you're good at coding and have a little business sense, you can live off your coding skills and not need to rely on anyone else. If you're really lucky, you can accumulate enough money where you can simply live off your investments.

Of course there are two sides to this equation, income and expenses. If you can keep your expenses down, making enough income to cover them is easier. If you've had a startup exit, then you may have a nice chunk of change at your disposal. If you invest that in a diversified way, you could probably live off that forever, if you can keep your spending to around 4 percent of your stash.

So what does that really mean? Let's say you had $1,000,000 in a brokerage account. If you put that in a low fee ETF (Exchange Traded Fund), then it would probably grow at about 7 percent per year. Assume an inflation rate of 3 percent of that per year, and you can spend 4 percent, that leaves you with $40,000 per year to live off. Hmm, that doesn't sound great at first. The average household income in the USA is currently at $60,000 per year. But that $40,000 per year is money you can spend without working for it.

There is now an entire movement called FIRE (Financial Independence, Retire Early). There are many takes on it, but basically people have realized they can live happy lives without having to work for *the man* until they retire at sixty-five. The FIRE folks focus on how to get the stash big enough to retire early, but also on living more economically. It turns out you can live very well on less money if you're thoughtful about it. Cutting out the $3 per day Starbucks habit is a start.

When I left Inktomi in 2001, I thought my stash was big enough that I could retire. Technically that was probably true had we been willing to severely cut back on the spending side of the equation. But I wasn't willing to cut my expenses back to the 4 percent level at that point. Living in California was fun but very expensive. Private schools for the kids were expensive. Our lifestyle was expensive. We could have cut back on our expenses, but it would have felt like a hardship at that point. Our stash wasn't big enough, so I kept working. After starting and selling Truveo, the stash was finally big enough. We could comfortably live off it.

But then what? What do you do when you don't have to work? My wife took up tennis and loves it. I tried but it didn't take. I didn't find it interesting enough. Sports are a great option. They provide a social network, something to do with your time, and they keep you fit. I like more solitary sports, like mountain biking, kite surfing, and snowboarding.

CLUBHOUSE EAST ASIA

After selling Truveo, we decided to move to Vietnam for a year. It was an exciting adventure. We sold our cars, put the California house on the market, rented our Nevada house, and moved to Saigon. We kept busy getting the kids settled in their new schools. We made new friends, got to know Vietnam, and explored Asia from our new base. But still in the end something was missing. I tried learning new programming languages, I blogged on a regular basis, I practiced my Vietnamese, but in the end I was still bored. I needed to be *doing something.*

I read a lot and watched every episode of *The Wire,* which was great. I remember running across a quote in *Wonder Boys,* by Michael Chabon: "Irv had rediscovered, as surprisingly few men do, that the secret to perfect male happiness is a well-equipped clubhouse." This really struck a chord with me. I needed a clubhouse. For me, I had always had some sort of clubhouse. For me, a clubhouse was a place where you worked on something and collaborated with others. In a way, startups were clubhouses. In Vietnam, I missed my clubhouse. I thought about joining startups there, but it just didn't feel right. It's no fun being in a clubhouse that isn't a good fit.

CLUBHOUSE SILICON VALLEY

Eventually, we returned from Vietnam, and I decided to build another clubhouse. When Tim and I started Truveo we would meet once a week and go over status and plan what we should be working on. I realized this was a good way to get things moving. My friend Peter had time for weekly meetings, so we started our Thursday calls. We discussed ideas and came up with tasks for each of us to explore each week. Having a weekly meeting was sort of a forcing function. It motivates you to get something done each week, so you have some progress to report on a regular basis. We made some progress, but Peter was still working full time and he was on the east coast, so my clubhouse felt a little empty. I needed to recruit some more members.

Eventually, I decided to try Craigslist. Generally Craigslist is free, but for job listings they charged $75. I splurged and posted an ad looking for startup co-founders. It turns out that in Silicon Valley this was like feeding breadcrumbs to pigeons in a park. Pretty soon you have more attention than you can handle. Most of it, not good. I was about to give up when I ran into Yacin Bahi. He was the perfect fit for me. He had startup experience, a PhD, liked to code, and in a weird twist of fate, his kids were in the same school as ours. Yacin had his own consulting company that he was running but wanted to be part of a startup that was building something new from scratch. Yacin and I started our weekly meetings.

Eventually, I was connected to Tom Sheffler, another computer scientist who wanted to give startups a try. Tom had worked for Rambus, a successful Silicon Valley company that made memory chips faster. His Rambus options netted him a financial cushion that could supplement his lifestyle while we worked on something new. At Rambus he was involved in hardware projects like the Sony PlayStation. We thought we might be doing something in hardware, so this could be helpful. Tom's PhD was from CMU, where I worked before moving to Silicon Valley. The clubhouse was filling up.

We were experimenting with different ideas around how to make sensors and cameras work for home automation. Around that time in 2009, cheap Wi-Fi connected cameras were showing up on the market. They were generally horrible to use but cheap. The nagging problem of watching my house while traveling was about to get much better. We decided to make a cloud service for security cameras. Sensr.net was born and I had my new clubhouse.

Of course, it was a virtual clubhouse, we didn't have funding or a real office. We met weekly at my house or maybe a coffee shop. It turns out my friend Fowler's startup Jigsaw had continued to grow and was now in fairly swanky office space a few miles away from the office where Tim and I had incubated Truveo a few years prior.

I asked Fowler if my new Sensr.net team could hang out at the latest version of the Jigsaw office.

"Yes, but on one condition," he responded, looking serious. "You can NOT have another exit before Jigsaw!" he broke into a laugh.

Truveo had started after Jigsaw and had been quickly scooped up by AOL when the internet video craze was just starting. Fowler had been steadily building Jigsaw into a substantial company while I was off working for AOL and then unsuccessfully trying to figure out how to retire in Vietnam.

Tom, Yacin, and I grabbed a couple cubicles in the Jigsaw office and started working away there. It didn't last long though; Jigsaw was growing fast and we had to move out.

Fowler got his exit when Salesforce acquired Jigsaw in 2010 for a reported $142 million.

About that time I heard about a thing called Sunfire Offices. It was another sort of clubhouse, this one funded by VCs. There was no rent, but if you were admitted, you just had to go to the weekly talks on Thursdays. The idea was to have a pool of highly-qualified entrepreneurs the VCs companies might want to hire. The weekly talks were more or less recruiting talks. It was a perfect fit for Sensr.net. None of us ended up getting recruited, but it was a good home for us for a while.

Sunfire was a very interesting experiment. It was an attempt to create a clubhouse of sorts. The idea was to bring together interesting and successful entrepreneurs from Silicon Valley. Give them a place to work and hang out. It was a co-working space, but with a couple of unique twists. First, the office space was free. You didn't need to pay to be a part of Sunfire. You did need to get voted in though. It wasn't a place for start-ups with funding. You had to be working on a pre-funded startup, or just an idea. The concept was to bring together like-minded people so they could collaborate.

Sunfire Offices were located in a swanky office building on Castro Street in Mountain View, the heart of Silicon Valley. Obviously there had to be some way to pay for the office space, and the model was to get VCs to foot the bill. Why would a VC foot the bill so a bunch of techies could hang out there for free? The argument was this group of elite individuals would be valuable to the companies that the VCs had already funded.

The members were all folks who were rockstars in some way. This was a highly sought after talent pool. Basically by funding the office, VCs had access to this talent pool. In the startup world, the most important thing is the team. You can have a great idea, but without a good team to make it happen, it won't matter. Conversely, if you have a great team, then they can come up with a good idea, even if their first idea turns out to be a dud. In startup vernacular, this is called a "pivot." Smart teams can pivot to new ideas.

Started in the summer of 2010, Sunfire was just what I was seeking. I had been working on Sensr.net with my co-founders Yacin Bahi and Tom Sheffler. We didn't have funding, but we did qualify for the "quality people" requirement of Sunfire. I read about Sunfire in *TechCrunch,* and I wanted in. My friend Vishal was a member. Vishal had worked with us at Truveo. He was now working on a new startup idea and hanging out at Sunfire. I pinged Vishal and he told me to come down and check it out. I would need to meet Niniane and Yishan, the founders of Sunfire. Vishal could nominate me, but they would have to approve me for membership.

I told them about what we were doing with Sensr.net and gave them our backgrounds. It seemed like a good fit for Sunfire. We were in.

At Sunfire, there were a bunch of shared office spaces and one common area with couches that was also used for the Thursday presentations. You see, if you were a Sunfire member, you were expected to attend Thursday afternoon presentations. These were sometimes led by members discussing their projects. It was also a forum for outside companies to pitch the members.

The Sensr.net team now had a place to hang out. We had free coffee. We had interesting people to chat with and bounce ideas off. I gave one of the Thursday talks, which included a demo of Sensr.net. I showed how you could view a security camera on the Sensr.net webpage. Using our site during the live presentation, I grabbed a snapshot from my driveway camera at our Nevada house and posted it to Facebook. The crowd applauded! Niniane asked if we could add some cameras to the office. Absolutely! We seemed to be onto something.

I was generally happy with the way things were going. I had formed a company and offered stock to Yacin and Tom. But eventually it became clear we needed some funding. Tom and Yacin could spend some time working only for stock, but it wasn't something they wanted to do for years. I was torn. I didn't really want to have to take funding. Funding really meant working for someone else. But I would probably lose my clubhouse members if we didn't try. So we put together a pitch and started our coffee meetings. Truveo had been a great success, so I started with our investors there. A few of them came in and that helped prime the pump.

I met Santo Politi back in the NeoPyx days, circa 2001, when he was at Charles River Ventures. In 2010 he had his own firm, Spark Capital, and they were doing great. We had discussed taking funding from Spark back in the Truveo days, but we were acquired instead.

Spark was Boston based and my daughter was just starting school in Boston, so I met him for breakfast while we were in town. He loved the idea and invited me back the next week to present to the partners. A week later we had a term sheet from Spark. They would put in $750,000 if I could get a matching $750,000. This reminded me of Red Swoosh, but it was different this time. I knew getting $750,000 from my investor network would be easy. About a month later we had $1.5 million in the bank.

I was excited I had funded my own startup, but now I had to really go back to work. What was I thinking?

WHERE ARE THEY NOW?

What lessons can we learn from those who have been through the startup experience? Some keep going. They thrive on the challenges of startups and have figured out the formula, so why not keep doing it? Others have found other passions and have focused on those. For some, they made enough money to have total freedom and can choose to do what they like with their time. For those that didn't make any bank, they have their own stories to tell.

DENNIS MCEVOY

As Inktomi started growing, we needed someone who had built engineering teams before. Dennis McEvoy was an experienced tech entrepreneur and in 1997 a respected Silicon Valley executive. Everyone at Inktomi believed the sky was the limit; that we were living in a new frictionless economy, and this time it would be different. Dennis aggressively sold his stock every chance he could, sometimes getting him in hot water with the CEO. Dennis enjoyed our enthusiasm, but he didn't drink the Kool-Aid. He had been around the block enough to know a bubble when he saw one.

Dennis taught us discipline and turned us into a well-oiled machine as we cranked out our software and satisfied customer demands for new features. After Inktomi dissolved into Silicon Valley history, Dennis and his tech entrepreneur wife decided to take a year off. They would detox from Silicon Valley. No board seats, no advisory positions, no angel investing. Dennis loves fast cars and took up track racing and car collecting. Golf became a passion.

He satisfies his love of competition by competing with himself. Can he beat his last track time or his best golf score? After a year of no tech life, he found that a satisfying life can be had outside the office. Successful retirement for him means continual challenges and intense focus on family, travel, and projects of his own choosing. He's a Tesla fan and peppers Elon Musk with questions at stockholder meetings. After a particularly hairy incident on the track, at his family's urging he decided to give it up, but he still drives fast. He meets with his golf coach weekly. *Always be learning* is a key to a successful retirement. For Dennis the detox worked, he found a way out of the Silicon Valley grind. For the other Inktomi alumni, it wouldn't be so simple.

PETER STEPHAN
After becoming a millionaire on paper with his Inktomi stock, Peter rode Inktomi down through the dissolution phase. He was our lead software engineer on site at AOL when Inktomi was being absorbed into Yahoo! AOL realized Peter was a valuable asset and took him on board. He's remained at AOL through the years, honing his networking and software skills. He's happy solving problems and

learning new things. Leveraging his master's in mathematics, he's focusing on machine learning these days. He participates in ML (machine learning) meetups and study groups where he often presents. Having worked for AOL for many years now, he's accumulated quite a lot of annual vacation, which he's sure to spend traveling with friends and family.

Peter and I still work a bit on keeping Sensr.net running but mostly those discussions are around how we ramp it down. We continue our Thursday calls when we brainstorm about startup ideas and keep each other up to date on our various projects. Perhaps we'll hit upon our next startup idea, but more likely we'll plan our next travel adventure.

JOHN PLEVYAK

After leaving Inktomi John tried to retire. He worked on the house and got involved in his kids' Montesorri school. But eventually he got tired of not working on interesting problems. "I became my wife's assistant, and that was no fun," he told me.

John has one of those brilliant technical minds, and it needs a challenge. Google recognized this and they hired him and put him to work, providing him with interesting problems and a fun place to go during the day. As a senior contributor, they started giving John a team to manage. John is not the manager type. He's more a Mad Scientist than Scientific Director. Now that Google adjusted his role, he's super happy churning out code and solving technical problems.

TIM TUTTLE

After we sold Truveo to AOL, Tim continued to grow and lead the team there for a couple years. He eventually left to start Expect Labs. As he had done with Truveo, Tim saw trends emerging around artificial intelligence and saw an opportunity there to build an AI-focused company. He used his skills as a startup entrepreneur to build Expect Labs and lead it through its acquisition by Cisco.

After building two very successful startups, Tim's taking a break and channeling his competitive spirit into tennis. He's a regular at the San Francisco Tennis Center. Tim plans to keep his knowledge up-to-date with advances in AI technology. He enjoys coding AI projects as a way to stay current.

JIM FOWLER

Post Jigsaw, Fowler jumped right in with another startup, first named Info Army, and then pivoted to Owler. Owler provides crowd sourced company intelligence. Fowler is also active on a number of company boards. After running Owler for a few years, he has stepped back from daily operations and is now focused on his passion for hiking, biking, and travel. Currently he's off on a five-month bike trip across Africa, from Cairo to Cape Town.

YACIN BAHI

After Sensr.net Yacin co-founded and ran iMuze, an AI music company. Yacin led iMuze through several rounds of funding and a pivot. He's currently the CTO of SAIFE, an AI company focused on detecting dangerous human behaviors.

Yacin continues to focus on his passion for building new technology and he's relocating from Silicon Valley to Puerto Rico, for reasons that will be clear later.

THOMAS SHEFFLER

After Sensr.net Tom took some time off to work on some passion projects around computer music and networking. He's created McLaren Labs as a way to focus his energies in this direction.

"Having mclarenlabs.com has been a nice outlet for me—a reason to learn new things and a place to have some interesting conversations with people. There's a guy in Japan who wants to play a sixteen-foot vertical piano in Belgium over the internet and he's going to try out my software. That's the new type of stuff I wanted to facilitate!" Tom told me in a recent email.

He worked at another tech startup before moving to Roche, the international pharmaceutical company, where he works as a Software Architect on their next generation gene sequencing platform.

SAMIR MEGHANI

Samir came along with the Truveo team to AOL and helped us do a major re-architecture of our search engine's back end, so it would scale better. After that, Samir was ready for another startup challenge. He founded Bountii, a shopping engine startup, and was accepted to Y Combinator, the prestigious Silicon Valley accelerator. After running Bountii for a few years, he joined me in an ill-fated startup called Dynamite Labs. We had an interesting app idea, but the timing just didn't quite work out. Snapchat filters came out, accelerating the death of Dynamite Labs.

Post Dynamite, Samir built his company, Cultivate, from scratch and is focusing on scaling it up. Cultivate continues to expand and gain market share. Samir has become a true serial entrepreneur.

MANY OTHERS

This is just a sampling of the folks I've worked closely with over the years. Some have continued to focus on building startups, while others have moved on to the relative comfort and stability of larger companies. Others have stopped working in the traditional sense, but are by no means *retired*.

There seems to be a relationship between age and work here that is interesting. If you've made enough money and you've figured out you can comfortably live off your investments and you're in your fifties, then it seems likely that you'll find other projects to keep you busy, rather than starting another company. If you're younger and are post-economic, then you tend to keep working the startup scene. My younger friends from Inktomi are still creating companies. The older ones seem to have found hobbies or other interests that keep them entertained. The key to a happy post-economic life seems to be finding something which challenges and interests you.

POST SILICON VALLEY

In my case, we decided to leave Silicon Valley behind four years ago and move to Puerto Rico. It was one of the best decisions we've made. For many people this would seem to be a risky decision. Puerto Rico is a Caribbean paradise but with quite a negative reputation. We have hurricanes, a bankrupt government, earthquakes, and a reputation for crime. As I write this the island is reeling from a series of powerful earthquakes that have caused over $100 million of dollars in damages and took out one of the major power plants on the island. Yet, I love living here.

Puerto Rico is exotic, but not too exotic. It was a Spanish territory until 1889 and retains much of that culture. But it's been a US territory for over a century and thus stable and familiar in many ways. Everyone born in Puerto Rico is a US citizen. You don't need a passport to travel to Puerto Rico. If you're a US citizen, you can move to Puerto Rico as easily as moving to any state.

Puerto Rico does have some major differences that make it different from a state. The government and laws are different from most states. For instance, the drinking age in Puerto Rico is eighteen, making it a popular destination for vacationing college students.

THE TAX THING: PART DEUX

As a US territory, Puerto Rico has interesting tax laws. If you live in Puerto Rico and make your income here, you don' t need to pay federal income tax, but you do need to pay Puerto Rico income tax, which tends to be lower than the federal rate. Most states have income taxes, but they don't replace the federal taxes, they add to your tax bill.

Another advantage of being a US Territory is the ability to write interesting tax laws. In 2012 Puerto Rico passed what is called Act 22 of 2012: Act to Promote the Relocation of Investors to Puerto Rico (Ley para Incentivar el Traslado de Inversionistas a Puerto Rico). This law was written to encourage investors to move to Puerto Rico by exempting them from most taxes on investment gains. The hope was that Act 22 would help reverse Puerto Rico's population decline and increase investment on the island. It seems to be working. If you meet certain requirements, you can receive an Act 22 Tax Decree which exempts you from paying capital gains tax on most types of capital gains. As a startup entrepreneur this is quite interesting. If you create a startup and sell it, this is just the kind of capital gain that is tax free under Act 22.

NEXT STEPS

My intention was to move to Puerto Rico and focus my energies on investments rather than building new companies from scratch. I spend my time advising startups through Parallel 18, a local startup accelerator, and serving on the boards of local tech companies. I'm also bringing a coding school to Puerto Rico to help increase the number of coders on the island.

I think it's critical to keep learning and challenging yourself. In my case, I'm focused on learning Spanish and I try to keep my hand in some coding projects as well. Once the coding school is up and running, I'm hoping to get back to building software again.

ARTISANAL STARTUPS

I became somewhat of an expert at creating and funding startups, but I've also learned this takes more effort and focus than I'm willing to devote to any one project at this point in my life. I enjoy the challenge and the camaraderie that comes from doing a startup, but it's just too intense. I've realized I'm just not motivated enough to put that much of my heart into it.

The main drawback to doing a traditional startup is taking other people's money. Once you've been funded, you now have someone else to answer to. I still come up with ideas that could turn into startups, but now I try to treat them more like Artisanal Startups, meaning a project I do for the love of doing it. I've found projects I think are viable businesses, but they could be done by me or in collaboration with a friend or two, and with almost no expenses. The goal in building an Artisanal Startup is to create something new and useful, but also to push yourself to learn something new. This fits the bill of continual learning and challenging yourself, a key to long-term happiness.

ACKNOWLEDGEMENTS

Writing this book has been a lot of fun. It all started at our weekly beach volleyball game in San Juan, Puerto Rico. We would hang out with our friends who are mostly from other places. As we got to know each other, conversations would often turn to our past lives and what we did before we moved to La Isla del Encanto. I would tell some of the stories you'll find in this book (and others that will never make into print). I would often get the response, "That's crazy, you should write a book!"

When my daughter Jade told me about Professor Koester's book writing class from Georgetown, I figured it was time to do it. I would like to thank Professor Koester for putting together the class and opening it to students outside of Georgetown.

I would like to thank my wife Loan for all her support during this process and for being my companion through this crazy journey from the academic world to Silicon Valley and now to Puerto Rico. I would like to thank my kids for their encouragement and putting up with my droning on about the writing course and the process.

Many thanks to my friends Peter Stephan, Tim Tuttle, Samir Meghani, Yacin Bahi, and Tom Sheffler, who accompanied me on many of these startup adventures and were gracious enough to let me include some of their stories here.

Finally, thanks to the folks at New Degree Press for pushing me along to the end. As we've seen, a key to living a happy life is making sure things are not *too easy*. It's important to challenge yourself. Like personal trainers who push you hard, but not too hard, the team at New Degree Press have kept me moving along with just enough structure and cajoling that I made it across the finish line.

EARLY CONTRIBUTORS

A special thanks to all the contributors to my Indiegogo campaign for Silicon Valley Stories. I probably wouldn't have done this without you all.

Adam Krim
Adrienne Bamford
Alan Burke
Allison Kern
Andrew Wick
Angelo De Giuli
Arjun Narayan
Bill Garner
Bill Moorier
Brian Marler
Brian Williamson
Carol Beguelin Parker
Chad Beguelin
Chris Robinson
Cuong Do
Dan Holloway
Dawn Brown

Carol and Karl Brown
Edward Robles
Evan Rose
Gary Nutt
Gert Degreef
Gino Rossi
Greg Lambert
Henry and Sandy Beguelin
Herbert Uhl
Jason Borseth
Jeff Clavier
Jeff McWhirter
Jennifer
Johnson-Wereszynski
Jon Vidar
Jonathan Brown
Jose Antonio Monti

Jose Otero
Joyo Wijaya
Karen Sperling
Kevin Brown
Lauren Cascio
Liz and Cornelius Bronder
Marc Bejarano
Mark Beguelin
Matt Melton
May Yam
Michael Cimarusti
Michael Starkey
Nancy K. Jones
Olivier Gillier
Orlin Goble
Pablo Averbuj

Paul Chiarappa
Paul Clip
Randy Ly
Rex Page
Richard Barrett
Richard Sheppard
Rudi Sanchez Colberg
Stacy Chiang
Tami Zhu
Timothy Tuttle
Tom Doulong
Tom Sheffler
Ty Martin
Vince Vannelli
Xiaodong Zhang

APPENDIX

NOTE FROM THE AUTHOR

Franklin, Bobby. "How big was 2018 for VC? Historic." *Venture Beat.* January 12, 2019. https://venturebeat.com/2019/01/12/how-big-was-2018-for-vc-historic/

Totty, Brian. 2020. User Profile, LinkedIn, accessed February 6, 2020. https://www.linkedin.com/in/btotty/

Brewer, Eric. June 22, 2004. *Inktomi's Wild Ride – A Personal View of the Internet Bubble.* YouTube. accessed February 6, 2020. https://www.youtube.com/watch?v=E910En1bnXM&t=2598s

INKTOMI INTERVIEW DAY

Wikipedia, s.v. "HotBot," last modified November 19, 2019, 13:38.

Internet Growth Statistics. "Usage and Population Statistics." Accessed on February 6, 2020. https://www.internetworldstats.com/emarketing.htm

Planes, Alex. "The IPO That Inflated the Dot-Com Bubble." *Motley Fool*. August 9th, 2013. https://www.fool.com/investing/general/2013/08/09/the-ipo-that-inflated-the-dot-com-bubble.aspx

Brewer, Eric. June 22, 2004. *Inktomi's Wild Ride – A Personal View of the Internet Bubble*. YouTube. accessed February 6, 2020. https://www.youtube.com/watch?v=E910En1bnXM&t=2598s

HOW DOES IT FEEL?

Brewer, Eric. June 22, 2004. *Inktomi's Wild Ride – A Personal View of the Internet Bubble*. YouTube. accessed February 6, 2020. https://www.youtube.com/watch?v=E910En1bnXM&t=2598s

HABANERO BURGER

The Habanero Hamburger "Hall of Flame", June 8, 2002. Accessed February 6, 2020. https://web.archive.org/web/20020608014318/http:/www.habanero-hamburger.com/

Made in the USA
Coppell, TX
11 May 2020